EASY PIANO
KELLY CLARKSON
GREATEST HITS • CHAPTER ONE

ISBN 978-1-4803-9367-7

HAL•LEONARD®
CORPORATION
7777 W. BLUEMOUND RD. P.O. BOX 13819 MILWAUKEE, WI 53213

Visit Hal Leonard Online at
www.halleonard.com

SINCE U BEEN GONE

Words and Music by MARTIN SANDBERG
and LUKASZ GOTTWALD

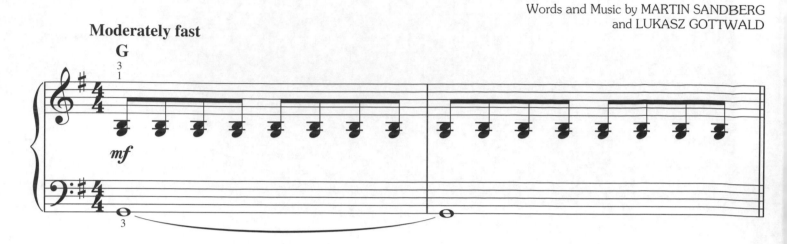

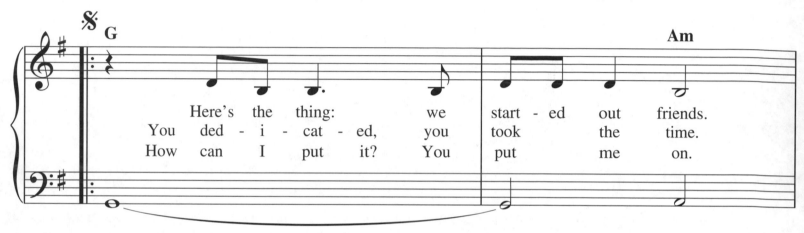

Here's the thing: we start - ed out friends.
You ded - i - cat - ed, you took the time.
How can I put it? You put me on.

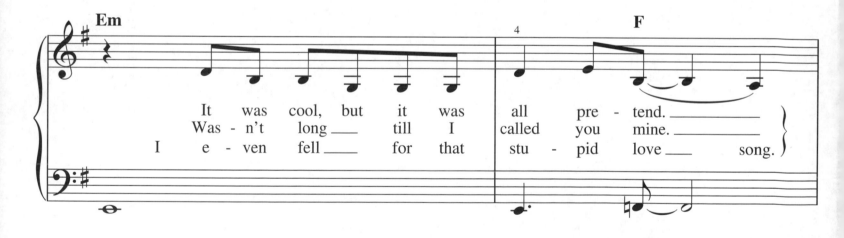

It was cool, but it was all pre - tend. ____
Was - n't long ____ till I called you mine. ____
I e - ven fell ____ for that stu - pid love ____ song.

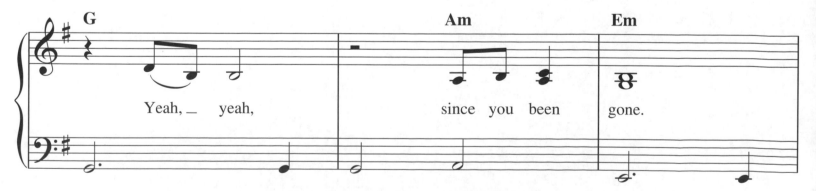

Yeah, ____ yeah, since you been gone.

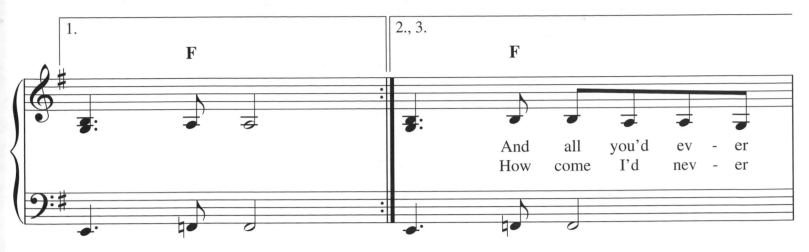

1. F   2., 3.   F

And all you'd ev - er
How come I'd nev - er

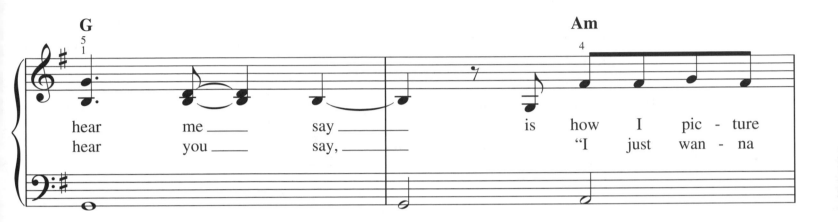

G   Am

hear me say   is how I pic - ture
hear you say,   "I just wan - na

Em   F

me with you.   That's all you'd ev - er
be with you?"   Guess you nev - er

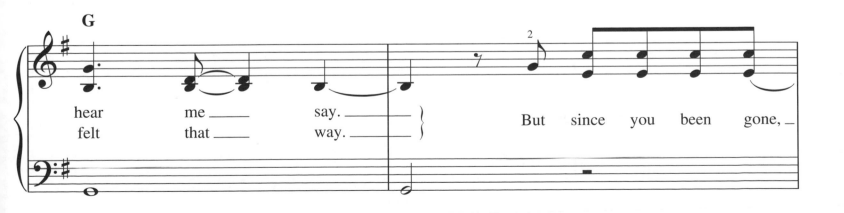

G

hear me say.   But since you been gone,
felt that way.

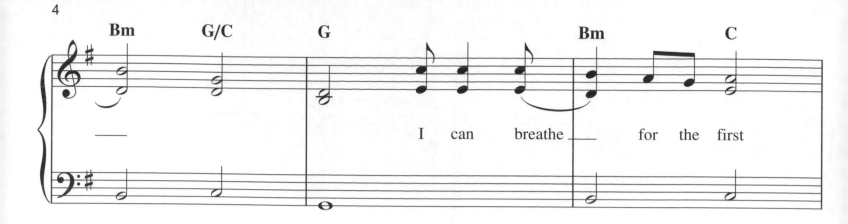

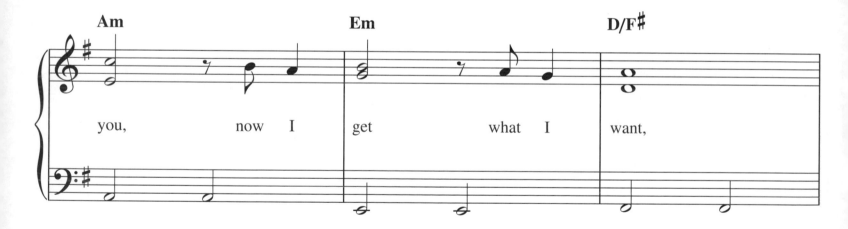

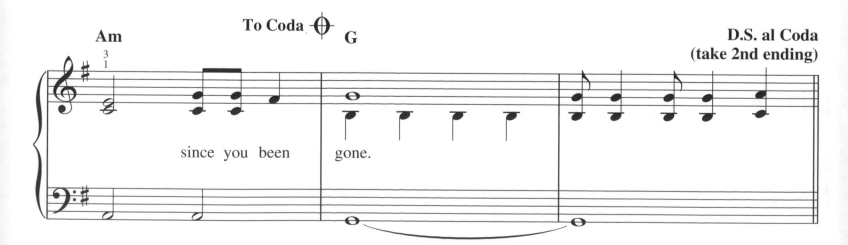

CODA

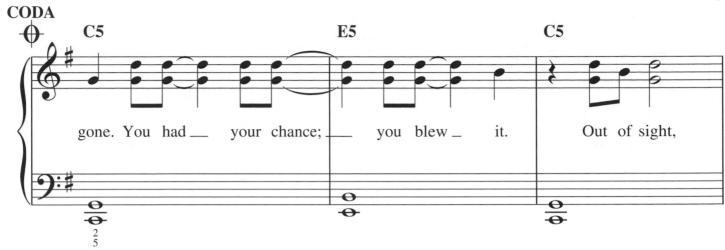

gone. You had your chance; you blew it. Out of sight,

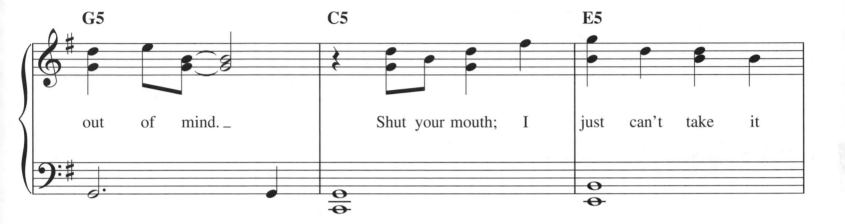

out of mind. Shut your mouth; I just can't take it

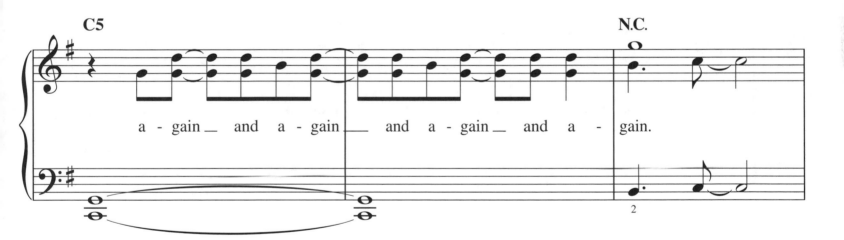

a - gain and a - gain and a - gain and a - gain.

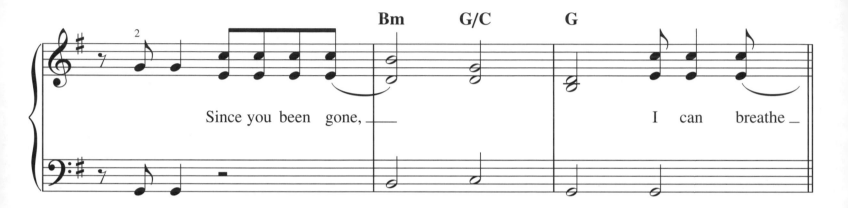

Since you been gone, _____ I can breathe _

_ for the first time. I'm so mov-ing on, _____ yeah,

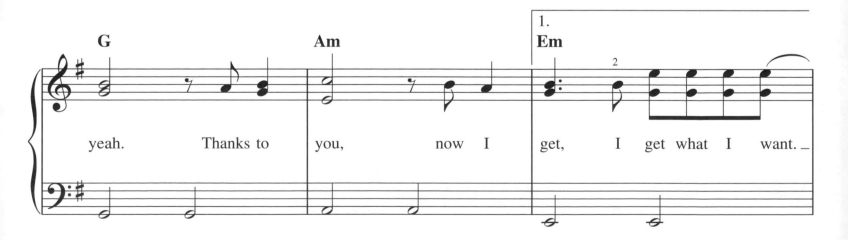

yeah. Thanks to you, now I get, I get what I want.

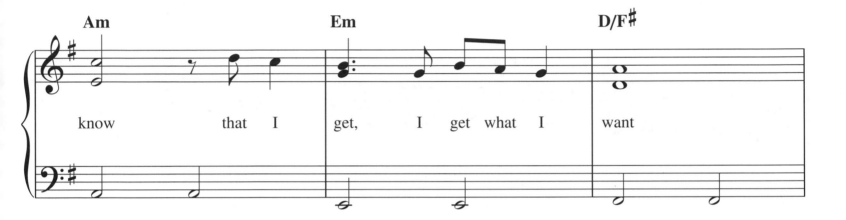

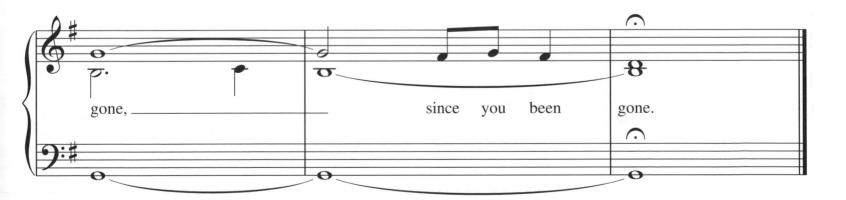

MY LIFE WOULD SUCK WITHOUT YOU

Words and Music by LUKASZ GOTTWALD,
MAX MARTIN and CLAUDE KELLY

Up-beat Pop

Guess this means ___ you're
May - be I ___ was

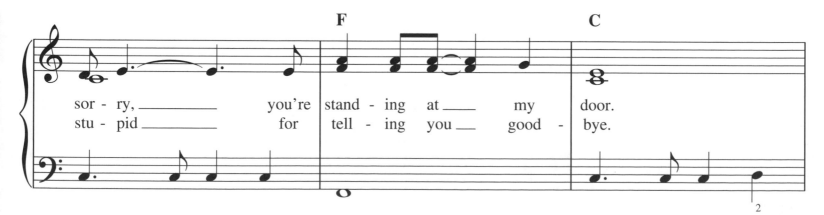

sor - ry, _____ you're stand - ing at ___ my door.
stu - pid _____ for tell - ing you ___ good - bye.

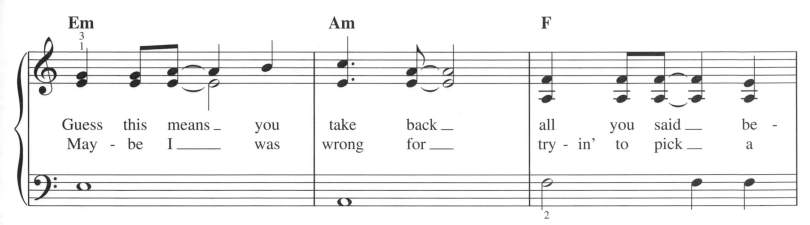

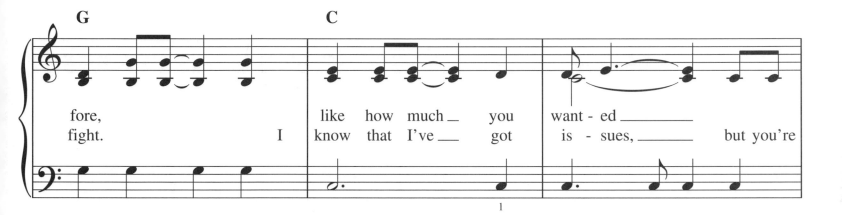

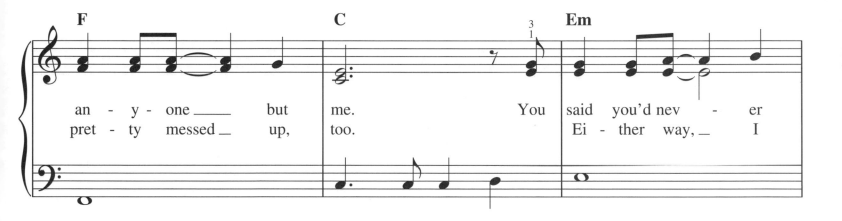

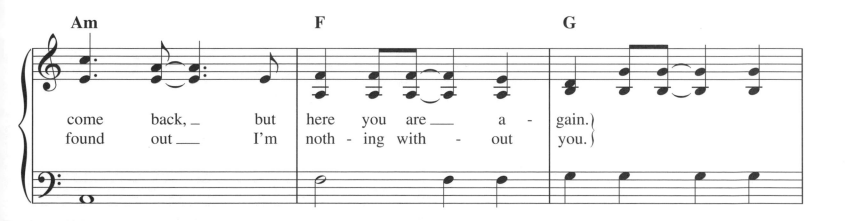

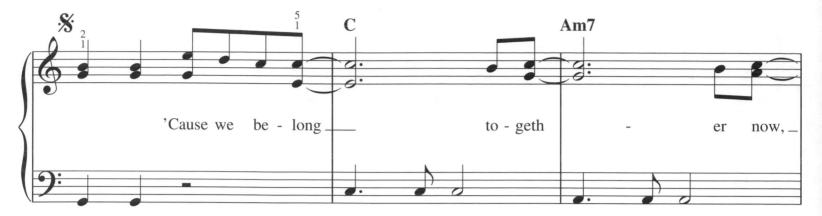

'Cause we be - long _____ to - geth - er now, _

_ yeah, for - ev - er u - nit - ed here _

_ some-how, _ yeah. You got a piece _____ of

me. And hon - est - ly, my

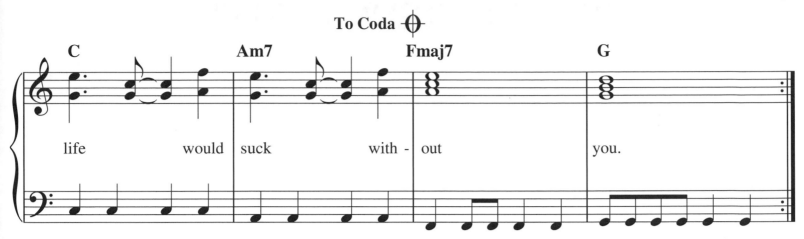

life would suck with - out you.

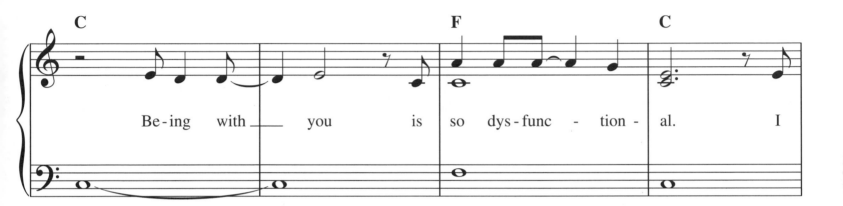

Be -ing with you is so dys-func - tion - al. I

real - ly should - n't miss you, __ but I can't let __ you go.

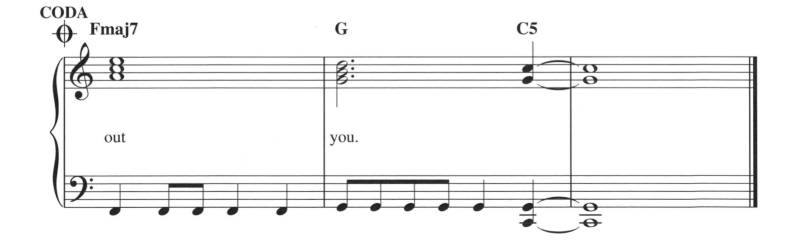

out you.

MISS INDEPENDENT

Words and Music by KELLY CLARKSON,
CHRISTINA AGUILERA, RHETT LAWRENCE
and MATTHEW MORRIS

Medium Rock

Miss Un - a - fraid._____ Miss Out - Of - My - Way.

Miss Don't - Let - A - Man - In - ter - fere,___ no._____

E9

Miss On - Her - Own._____ Miss Al - most - Grown. Miss

B9

Nev - er - Let - A - Man - Help - Her - Off - Her - Throne.__ So, by

14

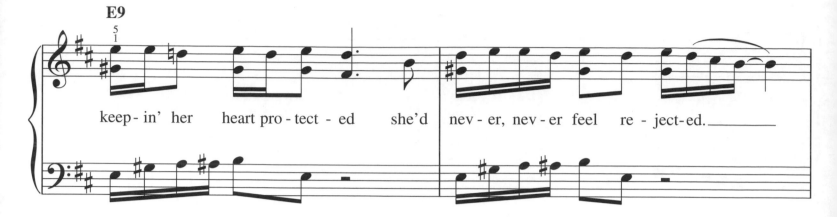

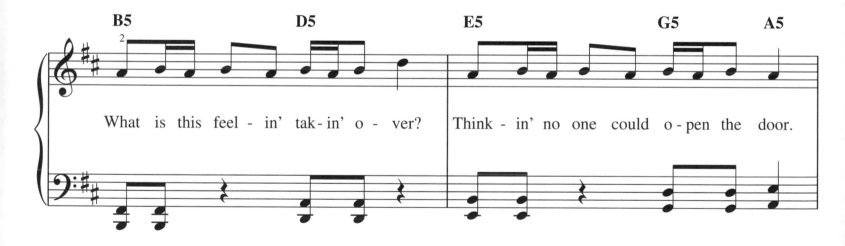

Not - Start, no._____ But she mis-cal - cu - lat - ed.__

__ She did-n't wan-na end up jad - ed and this Miss de-cid - ed not to

E9

miss out on true love.__ So by chang - in' the mis-con-cep - tions she

went in a new di - rec - tion and found in - side__ she felt a con-nec - tion.

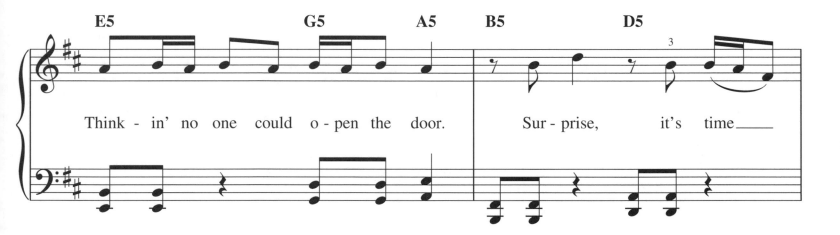

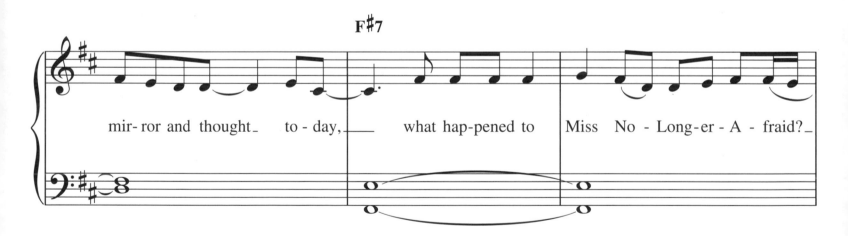

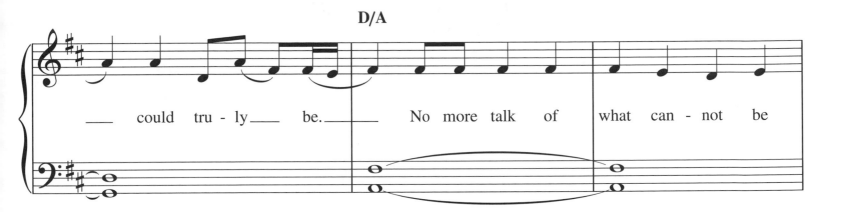

D/A

_ could tru - ly _ be. _ No more talk of what can - not be

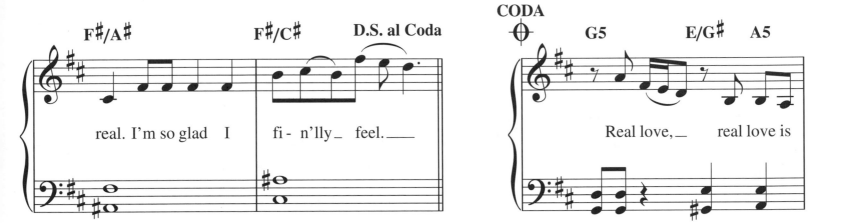

F♯/A♯   **F♯/C♯**   **D.S. al Coda**   **CODA**   **G5**   **E/G♯**   **A5**

real. I'm so glad I fi - n'lly _ feel. _   Real love, _ real love is

B9

true.

Miss In - de - pen - dent.

STRONGER
(What Doesn't Kill You)

Words and Music by GREG KURSTIN,
JORGEN ELOFSSON, DAVID GAMSON
and ALEXANDRA TAMPOSI

Moderate Dance groove

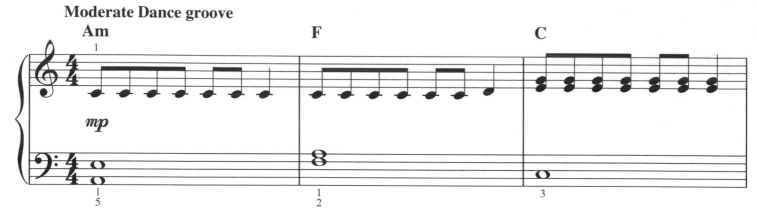

You know the bed feels warm - er _____

sleep - in' here a - lone. You know I dream in

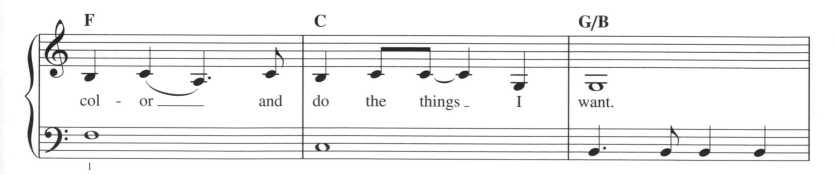

col - or _____ and do the things _ I want.

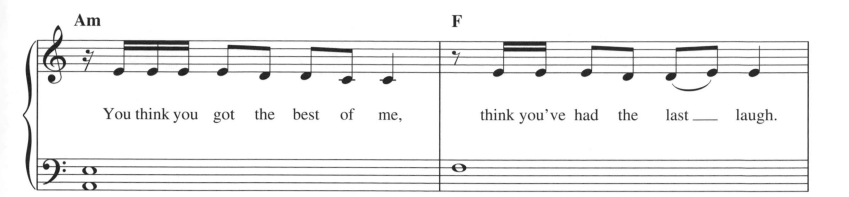

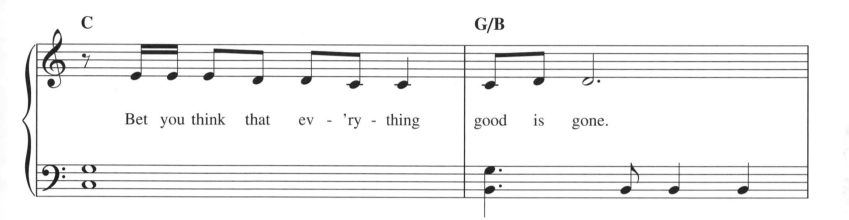

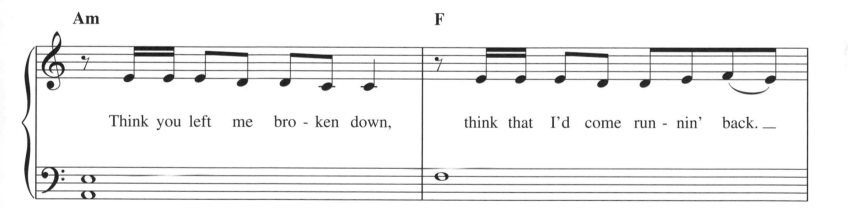

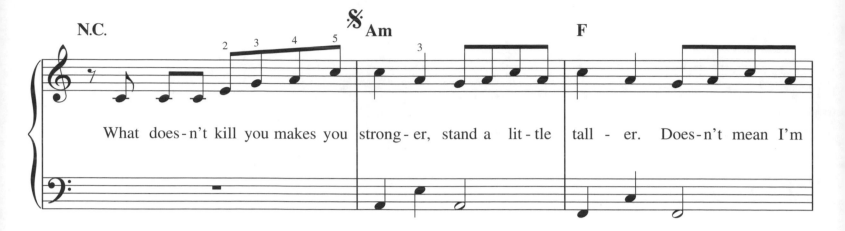

What does-n't kill you makes you strong - er, stand a lit - tle tall - er. Does-n't mean I'm

lone - ly when I'm a-lone. What does-n't kill you makes a fight - er, foot-steps e - ven

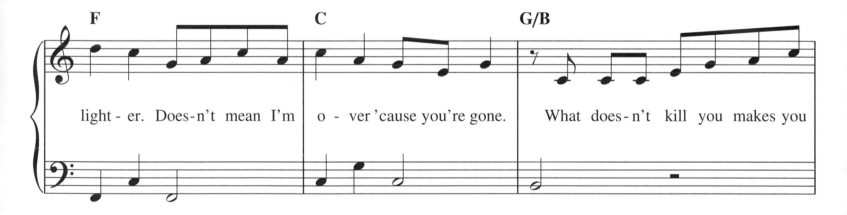

light - er. Does-n't mean I'm o - ver 'cause you're gone. What does-n't kill you makes you

strong - er, strong - er, _____ just me, my - self _____ and I.

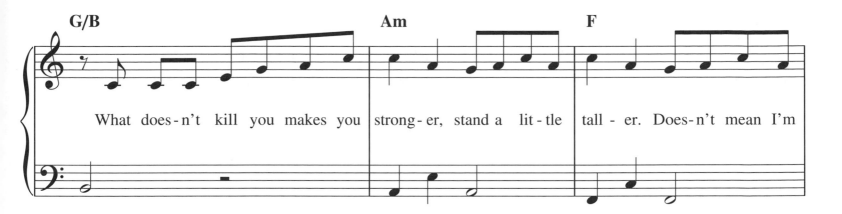

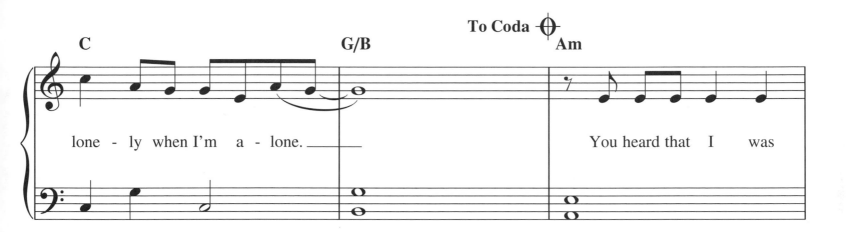

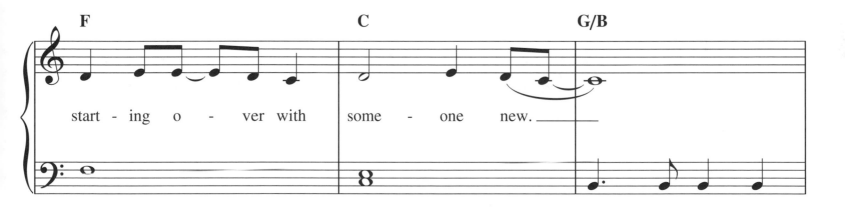

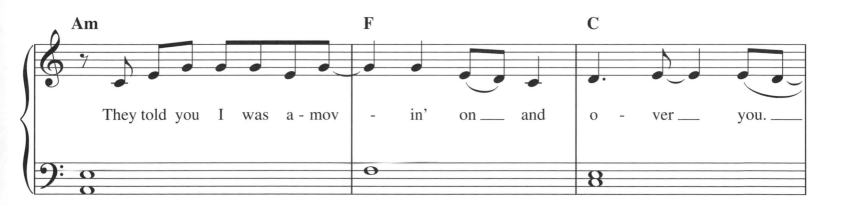

G/B   Am   F

You did-n't think that I'd come back,   I'd come back swing - in'.

C   G/B   N.C.   **D.S. al Coda**

You tried to break me. But you   see, what does - n't kill you makes you

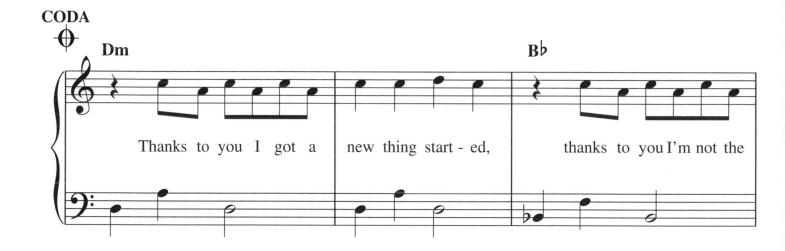

CODA

Dm   B♭

Thanks to you I got a   new thing start - ed,   thanks to you I'm not the

Am

bro - ken - heart - ed. __   Thanks to you I'm fi - n'ly   think- in' 'bout me.   You

F .... Am

know in the end, __ the day I left was just-a my be-gin-ning. _____

F .... C .... N.C. .... Am

In the _ end, _____ what does-n't kill you makes you strong-er, stand a lit-tle

F .... C .... G/B

tall - er. Does-n't mean I'm lone-ly when I'm a-lone. What does-n't kill you makes a

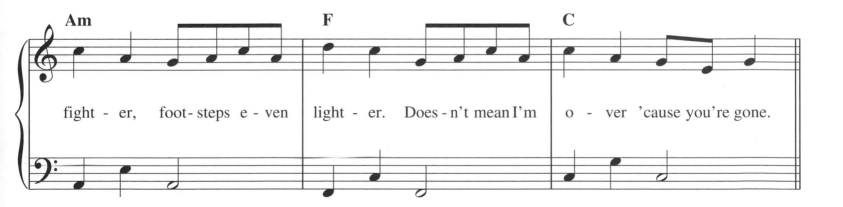

Am .... F C

fight-er, foot-steps e-ven light-er. Does-n't mean I'm o-ver 'cause you're gone.

26

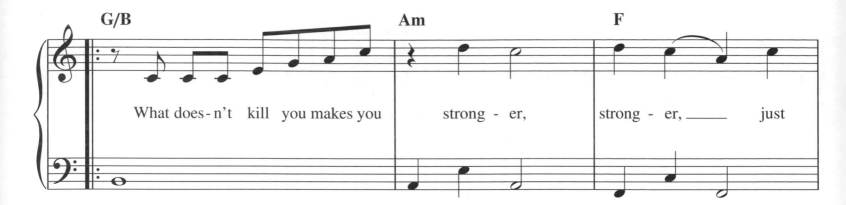

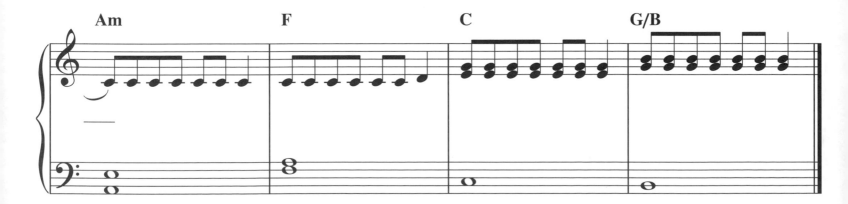

BEHIND THESE HAZEL EYES

Words and Music by KELLY CLARKSON,
LUKASZ GOTTWALD and MAX MARTIN

Seems like just yes - ter - day
I told you ev - 'ry - thing,

you were a part of me.
opened up and let you in.

I used to stand so tall; I
You made me feel all right for

used to be so strong.
once___ in my life.

Your arms a - round me tight,
Now all that's left of me

28

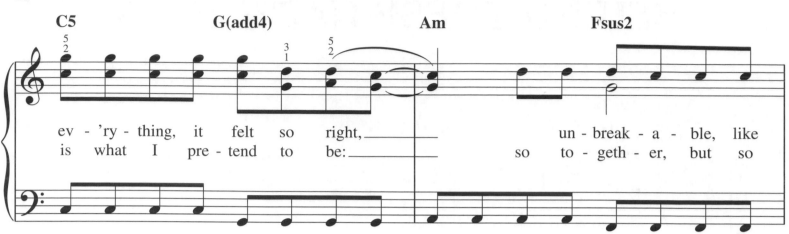

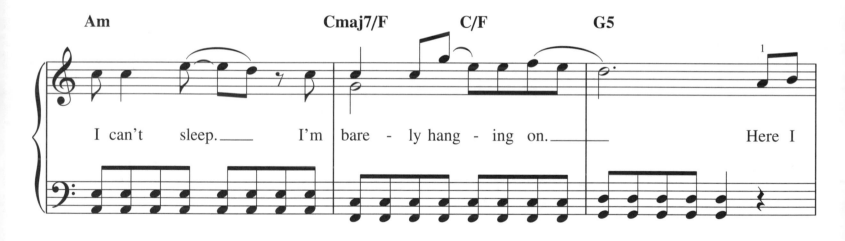

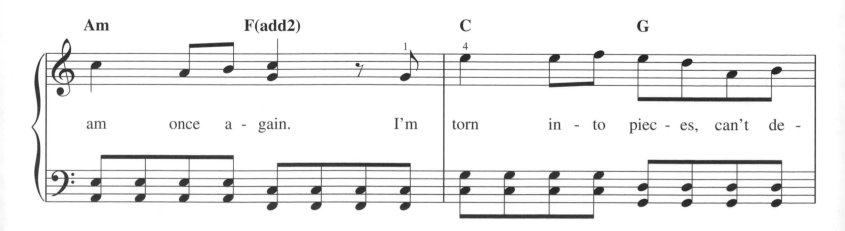

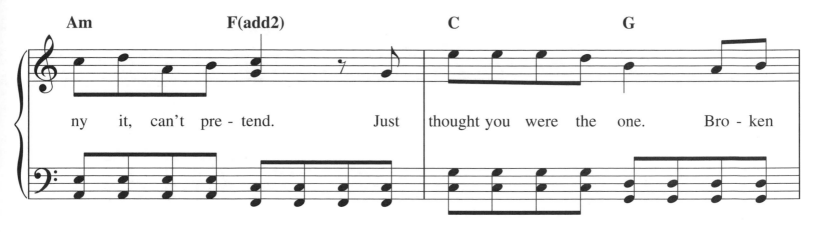

Am   F(add2)   C   G

ny it, can't pre - tend.   Just thought you were the one.   Bro - ken

Am   F(add2)   D5

up deep in - side,   but you won't get to see the tears I

Am   F(add2)   1. C   G

cry   be - hind these ha - zel eyes.

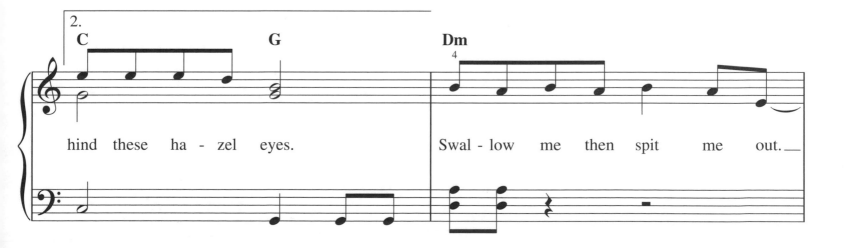

2. C   G   Dm

hind these ha - zel eyes.   Swal - low me then spit me out.

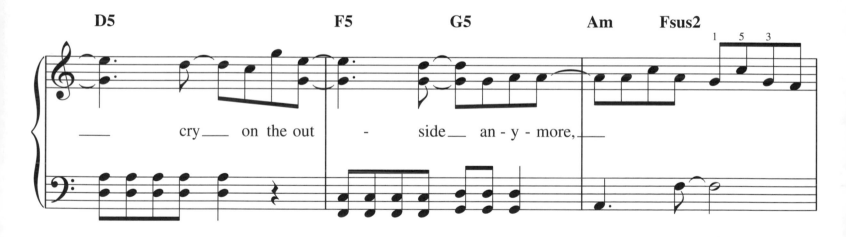

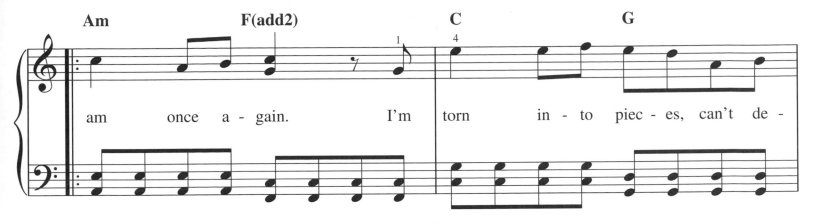

am   once a - gain.   I'm   torn   in - to piec - es, can't de -

ny   it, can't pre - tend.   Just   thought you were the one.   Bro - ken

up   deep in - side,   but   you won't get to see the tears I

cry   be - hind these ha - zel eyes.   Here I   hind these ha - zel eyes.

BECAUSE OF YOU

Words and Music by KELLY CLARKSON,
DARID HODGES and BEN MOODY

Words and Music by KELLY CLARKSON, DAVID HODGES and BEN MOODY

Moderately slow

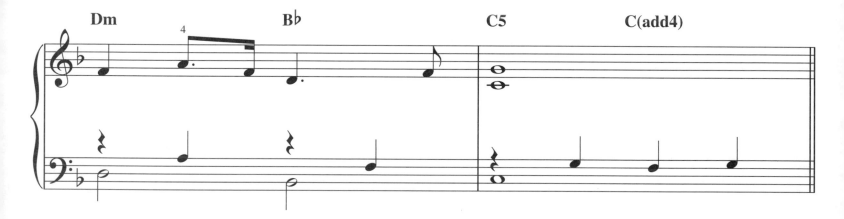

I will not make the same mis-takes that you did. I_____

I lose my way, and it's not too long__ be-fore you point_ it

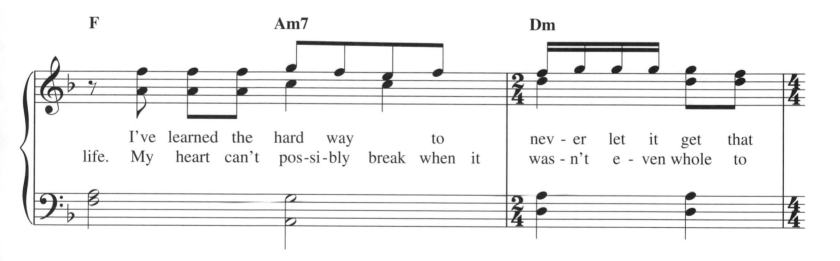

34

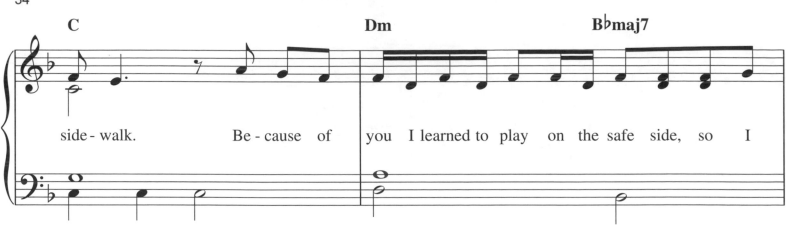

side - walk. Be - cause of you I learned to play on the safe side, so I

don't get hurt. Be - cause of you I find it hard to trust not on - ly

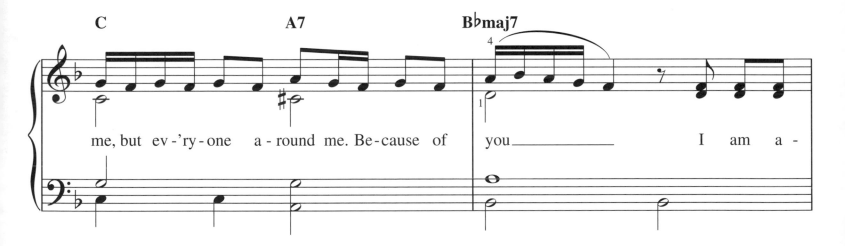

me, but ev - 'ry - one a - round me. Be - cause of you____ I am a -

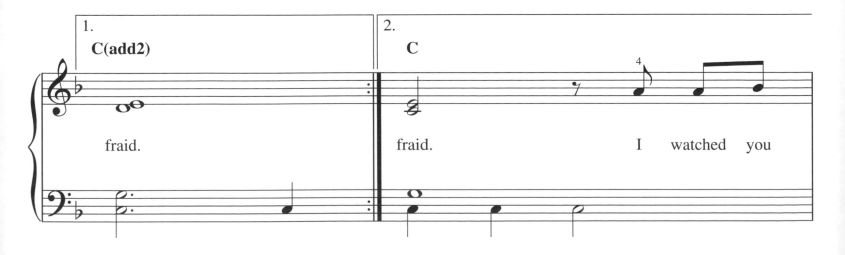

1.
C(add2)

fraid.

2.
C

fraid. I watched you

35

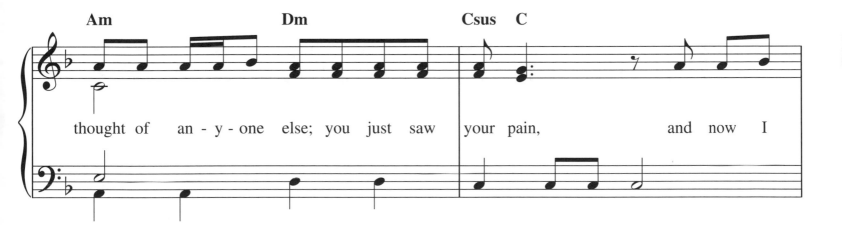

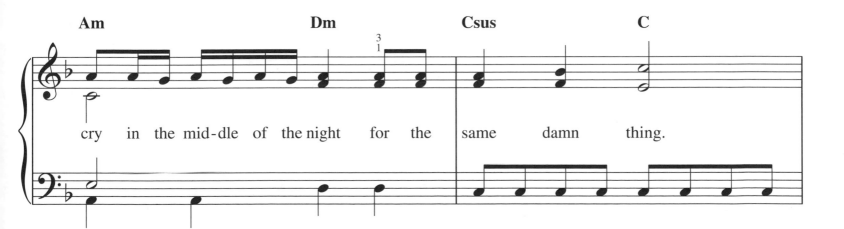

36

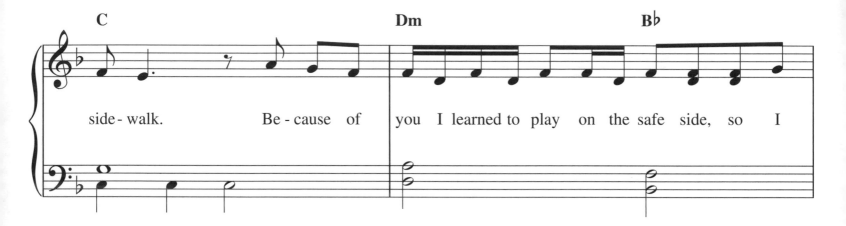

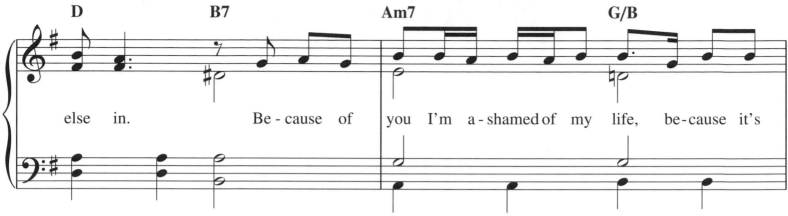

else in.   Be - cause of you I'm a-shamed of my life, be-cause it's

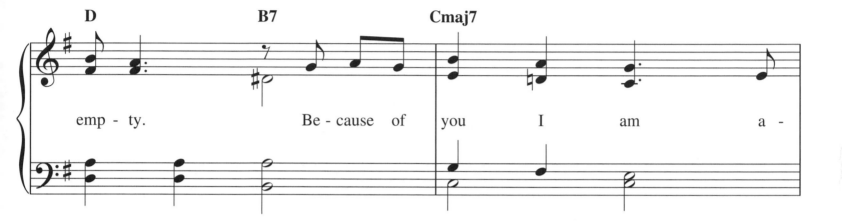

emp - ty.   Be - cause of you I am a -

fraid.   Be-cause of you,   be-cause of

you. _____   *rit.*

NEVER AGAIN

Words and Music by KELLY CLARKSON
and JIMMY MESSER

things, but I don't wish you well. Could you tell___ by the flames___

___ that burned___ your words?_____ I nev - er read___ your

let - ter 'cause I knew what you'd say.___ Gim-me that Sun-day school

an - swer, try and make it all___ o - kay. Does it hurt___ to know I'll

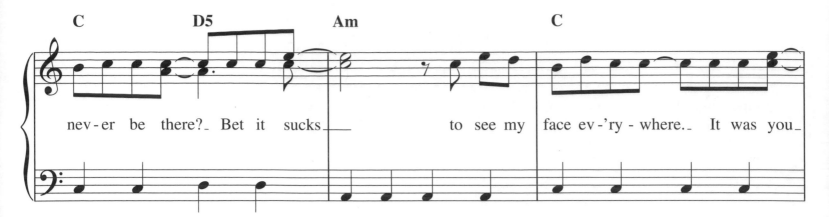

41

If she real - ly knows the truth, she de - serves ___ you.   A tro - phy wife,

oh, how   cute.   Ig - no - rance ___ is   bliss.   But when

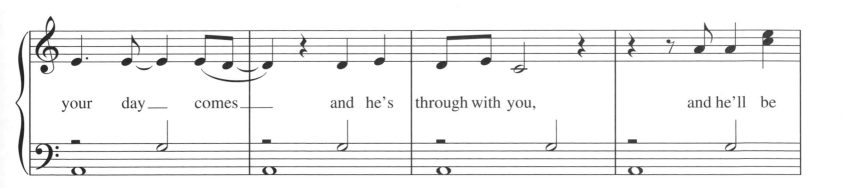

your day ___ comes ___   and he's through with you,   and he'll be

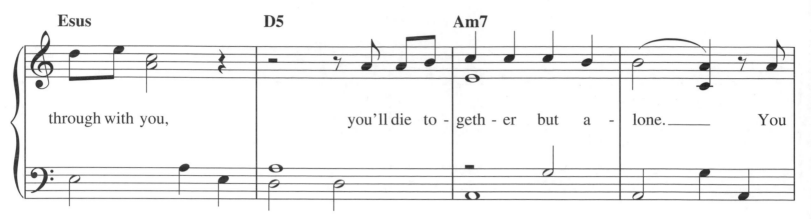

through with you, you'll die to - geth - er but a - lone._____ You

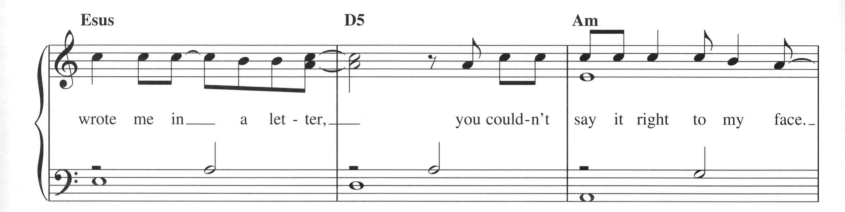

wrote me in_____ a let - ter,_____ you could-n't say it right to my face.____

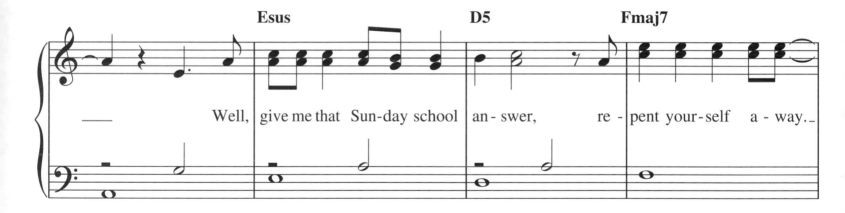

_____ Well, give me that Sun-day school an - swer, re - pent your-self a - way._

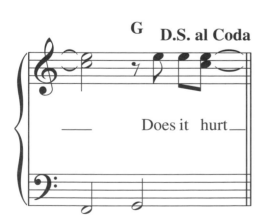

_____ Does it hurt____

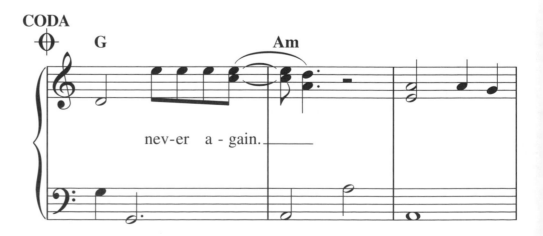

nev-er a - gain._____

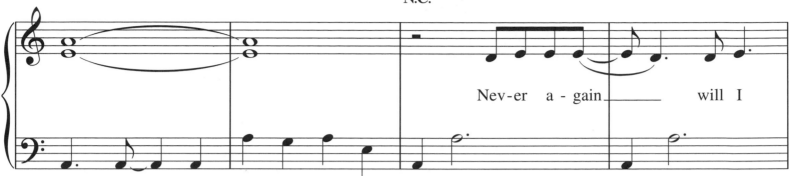

N.C.

Nev-er a - gain _____ will I

hear you. Nev-er a - gain _____ will I miss you. Nev-er a - gain _____

Am

will I fall to you, nev - er. Nev-er a - gain _____

Am7   Am6   F/A

_____ will I kiss you. Nev-er a - gain _____ will I

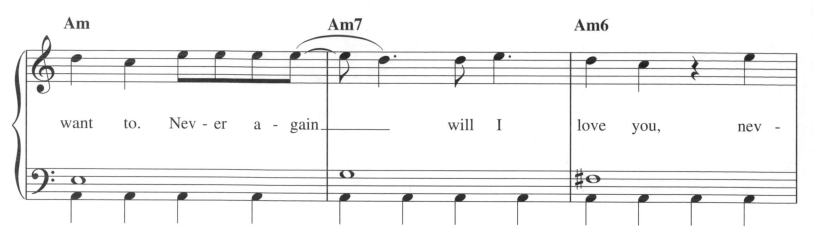

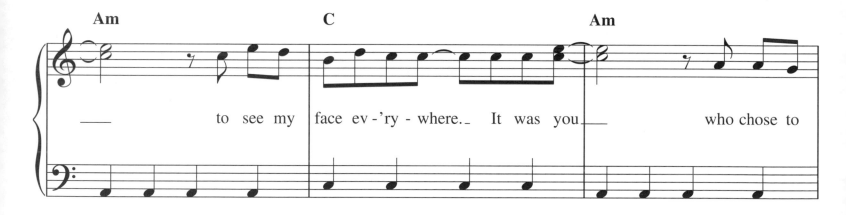

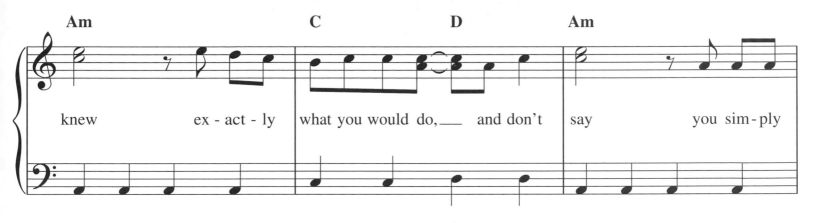

knew   ex - act - ly   what you would do, ___ and don't   say   you sim - ply

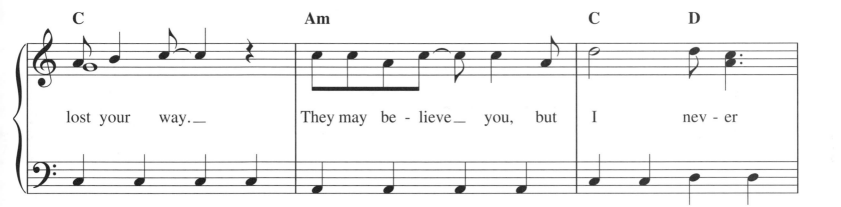

lost your   way. ___   They may be - lieve ___ you, but   I   nev - er

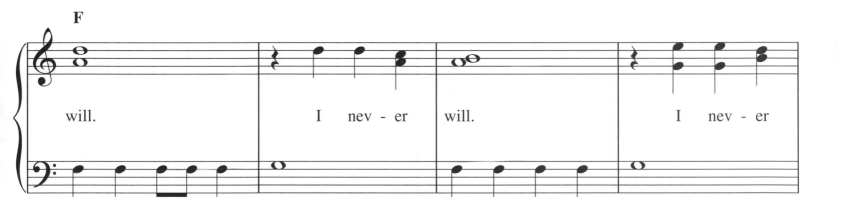

will.   I   nev - er   will.   I   nev - er

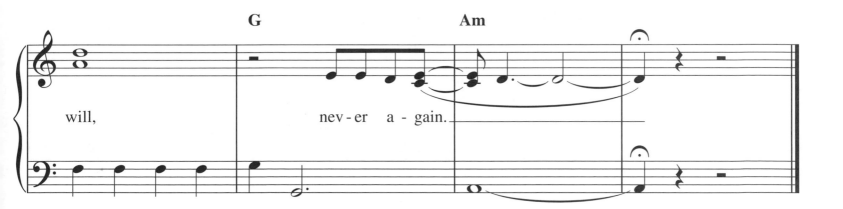

will,   nev - er a - gain. ___

ALREADY GONE

Words and Music by KELLY CLARKSON
and RYAN TEDDER

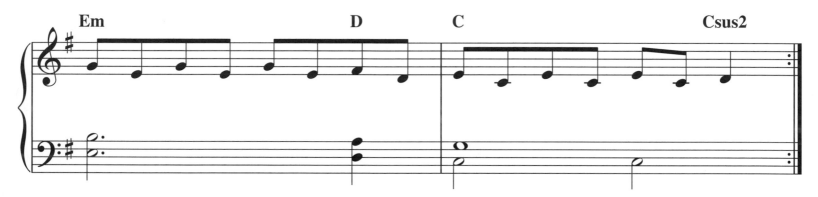

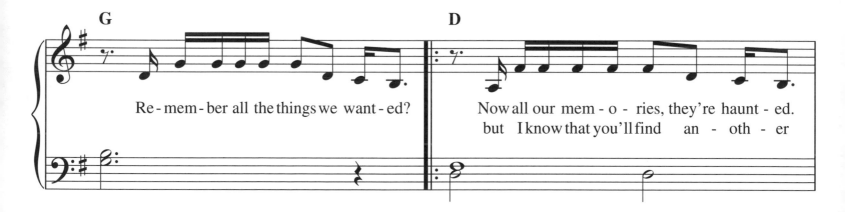

Re-mem-ber all the things we want-ed?

Now all our mem-o-ries, they're haunt-ed.
but I know that you'll find an-oth-er

We were al-ways meant to say good-bye.
that does-n't al-ways make you wan-na cry.

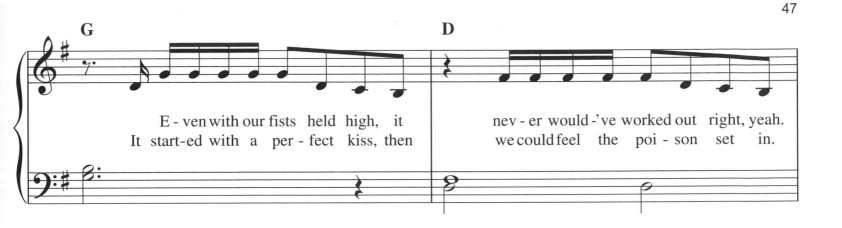

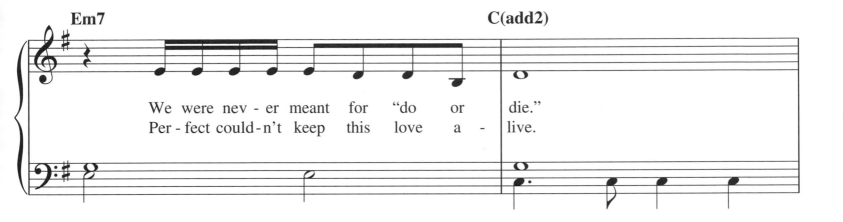

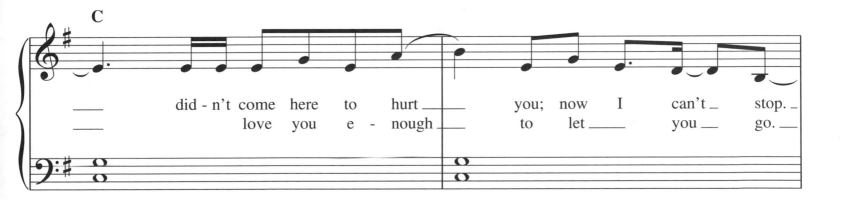

I want you __ to know that it does - n't mat -

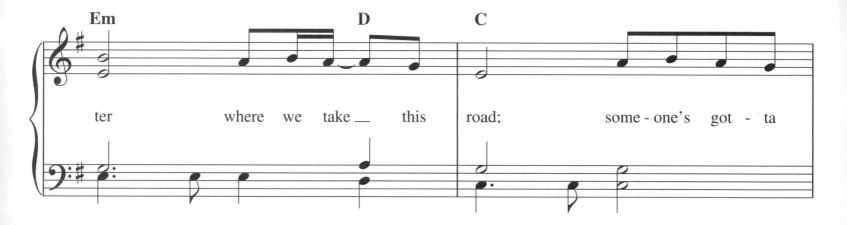

ter where we take __ this road; some - one's got - ta

go. And I want you __ to know, you could-n't have loved me

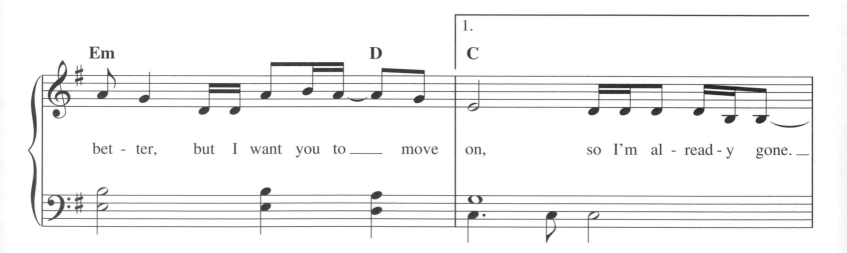

bet - ter, but I want you to __ move on, so I'm al - read - y gone.

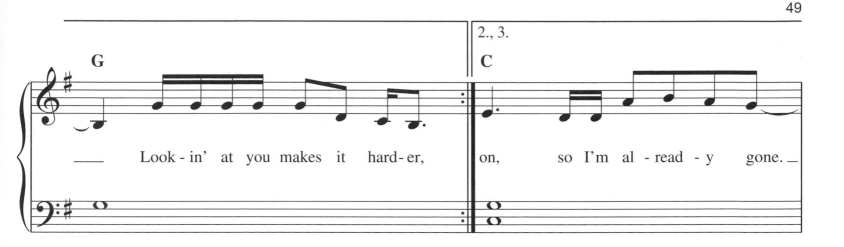

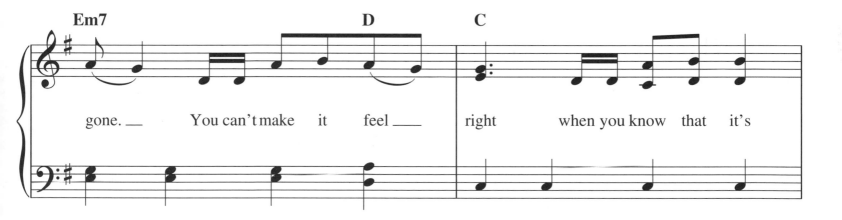

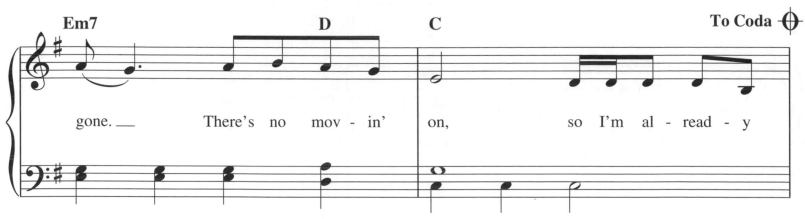

Em7   D   C   To Coda

gone. ___ There's no mov - in'   on,   so I'm al - read - y

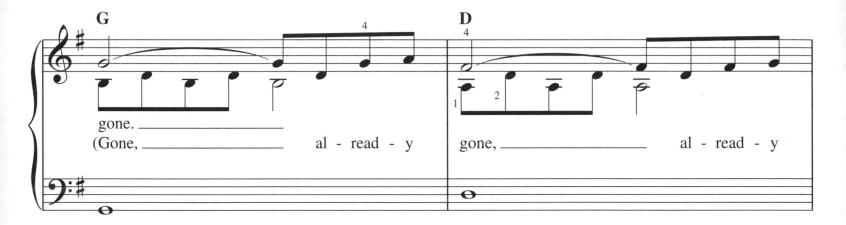

G   D

gone. _____

(Gone, _____ al - read - y   gone, _____ al - read - y

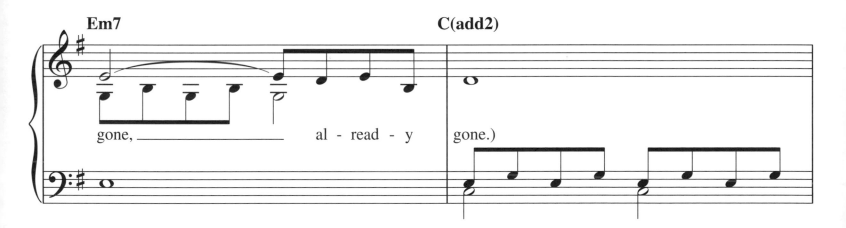

Em7   C(add2)

gone, _____ al - read - y   gone.)

G   D

(Gone, _____ al - read - y   gone, _____ al - read - y

gone, _____ al - read - y gone.)

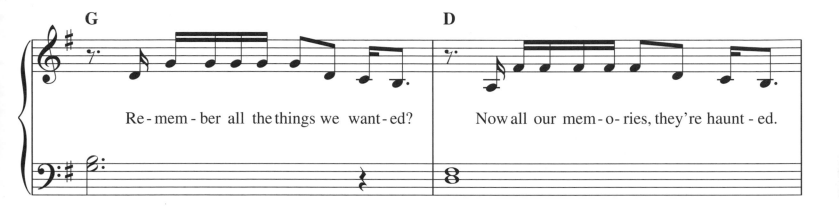

Re - mem - ber all the things we want - ed? Now all our mem - o - ries, they're haunt - ed.

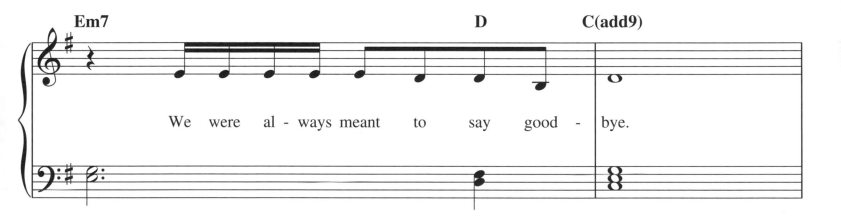

We were al - ways meant to say good - bye.

I want you ____ to

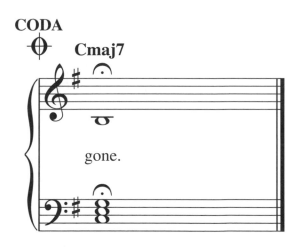

gone.

MR. KNOW IT ALL

Words and Music by ESTHER DEAN,
BRIAN SEALS, BRETT JAMES
and DANTE JONES

some-bod-y tells you some-thing 'bout you, think that they know you more than you do. So you

take it down, an-oth-er pill to swal-low.

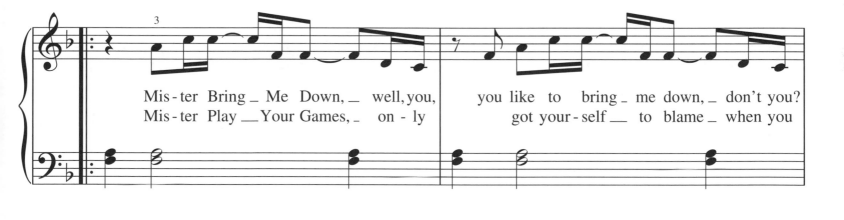

Mis-ter Bring _ Me Down, _ well, you, you like to bring _ me down, _ don't you?
Mis-ter Play _ Your Games, _ on-ly got your-self _ to blame _ when you

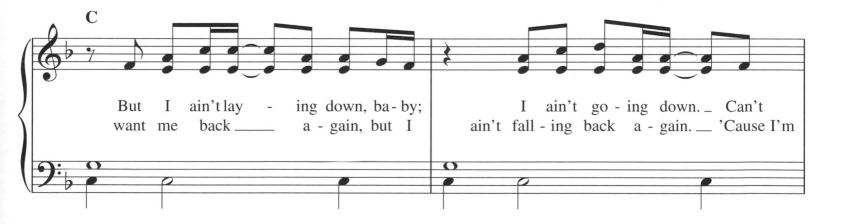

But I ain't lay - ing down, ba-by; I ain't go-ing down. _ Can't
want me back _____ a - gain, but I ain't fall-ing back a - gain. _ 'Cause I'm

54

no-bod-y tell me how it's gon-na be, no-bod-y gon-na make a fool out of me. Ba-by,
liv-ing my truth with-out _ your _ lies. Let's be _ clear: _ Ba-by, this is good-bye.

you should know that I lead, not fol-low.
I ain't com-ing _ back to-mor-row.
Oh, you think that you know _

_ me, know _ me, that's why I'm leav-ing you lone - ly, lone - ly.

'Cause, ba - by, you don't know a thing a - bout me, _ you don't know a

thing a - bout me. _____ You ain't got the right to tell me

when and where to go, no right to tell me. Act-ing like you own me, late - ly.

To Coda ⊕

Yeah, ba - by, you don't know a thing a - bout me, _____ you don't know a

thing a - bout me. _____

56

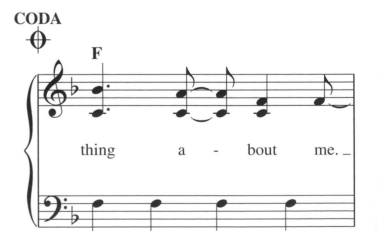

Mis - ter Know It All, ___ well, you,

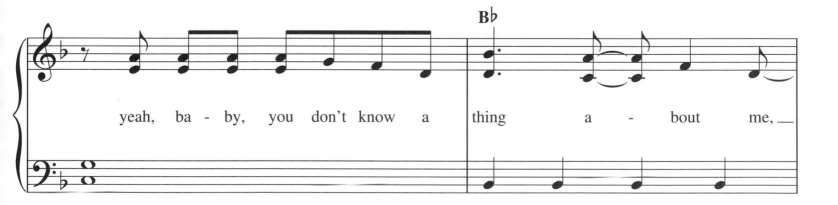

you think you know _ it all, ___ but you don't know a thing _ at all. Ain't you,

yeah, ba - by, you don't know a thing a - bout me, ___

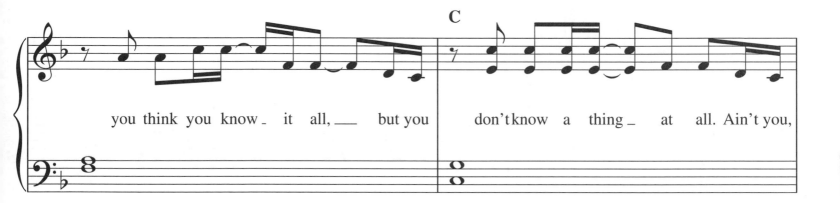

___ you don't know a thing a - bout me. ___

BREAKAWAY
from THE PRINCESS DIARIES 2: ROYAL ENGAGEMENT

Words and Music by BRIDGET BENENATE,
AVRIL LAVIGNE and MATTHEW GERRARD

Moderately

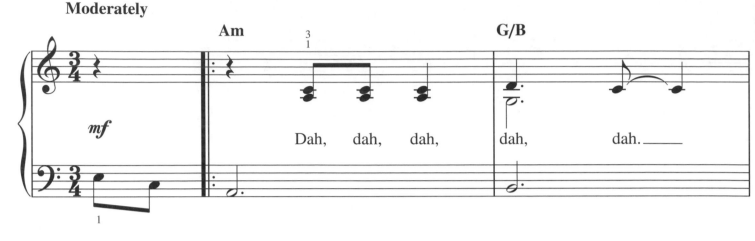

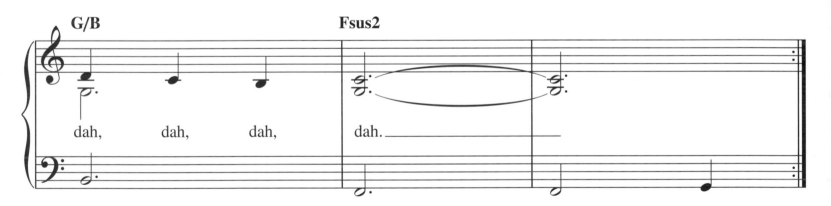

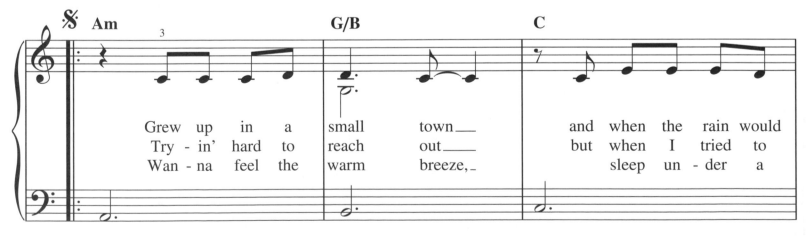

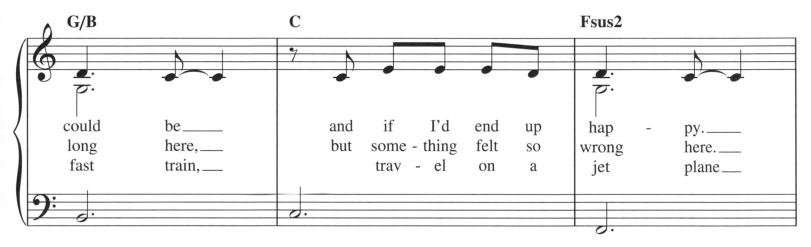

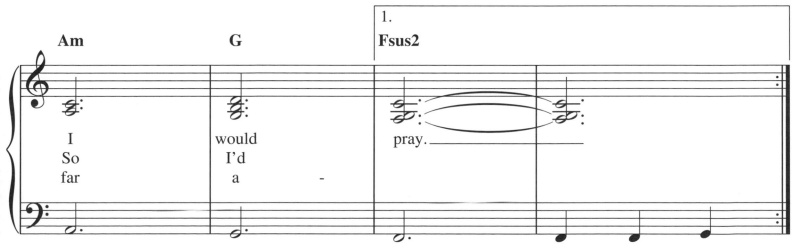

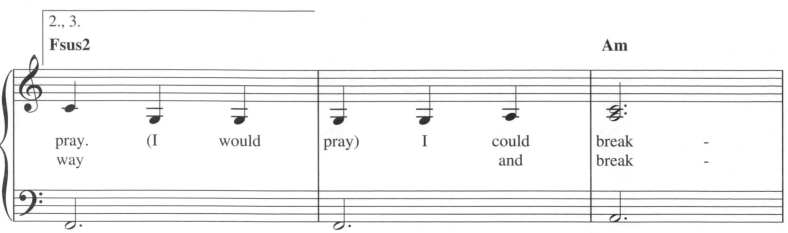

2., 3.

Fsus2   **Am**

pray.   (I   would   pray)   I   could   break -
way   and   break -

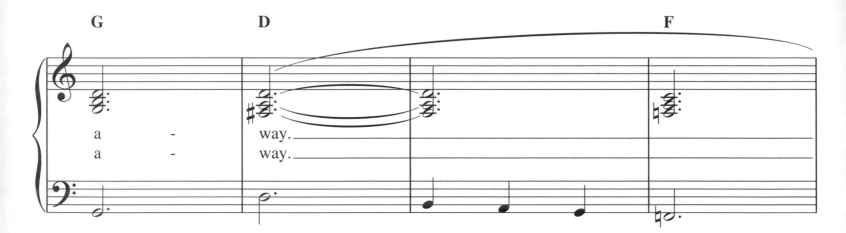

G   **D**   **F**

a   -   way.
a   -   way.

G   **C**   **G/B**

I'll   spread   my   wings   and   I'll   learn   how   to
Out   of   the   dark - ness   and   in - to   the

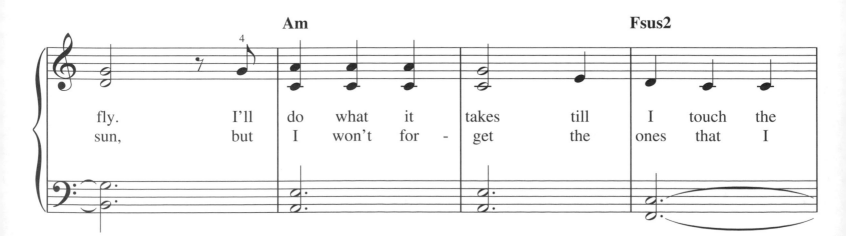

Am   **Fsus2**

fly.   I'll   do   what   it   takes   till   I   touch   the
sun,   but   I   won't   for - get   the   ones   that   I

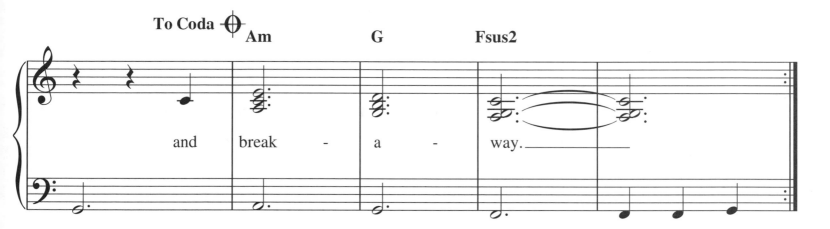

CODA

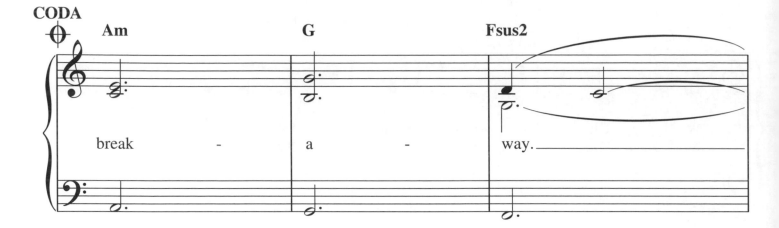

break - a - way.____

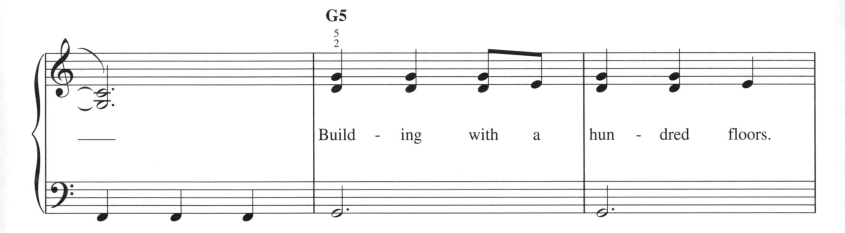

____ Build - ing with a hun - dred floors.

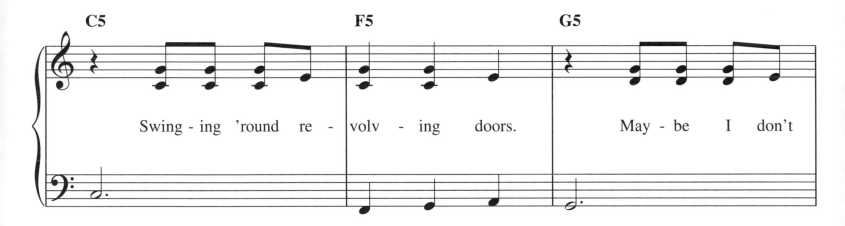

Swing - ing 'round re - volv - ing doors. May - be I don't

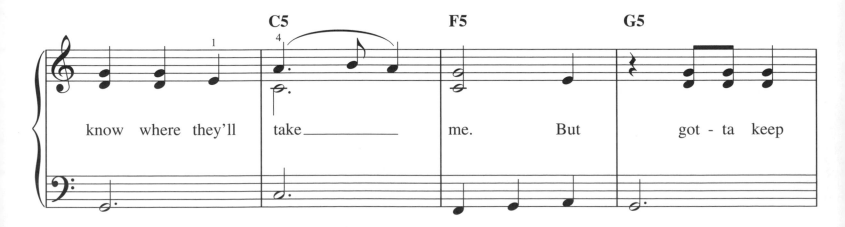

know where they'll take_____ me. But got - ta keep

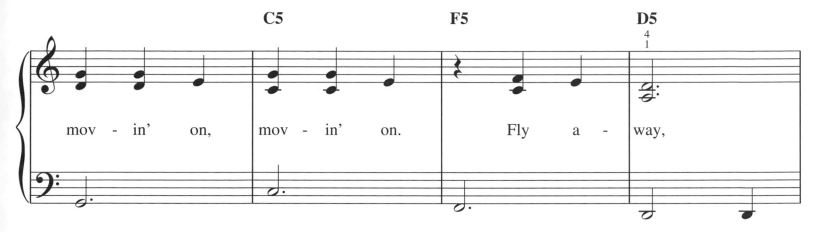

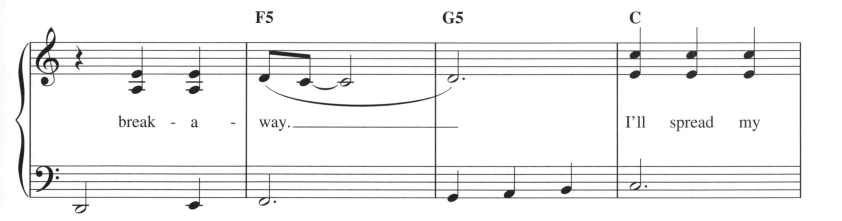

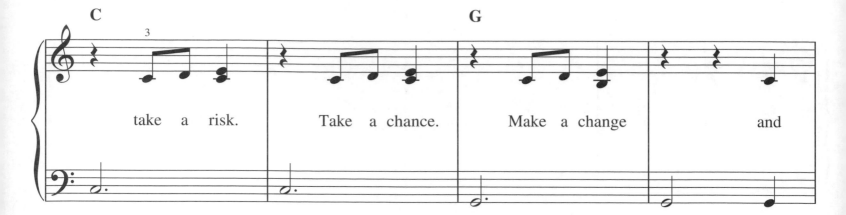

C   **G**

take a risk.   Take a chance.   Make a change   and

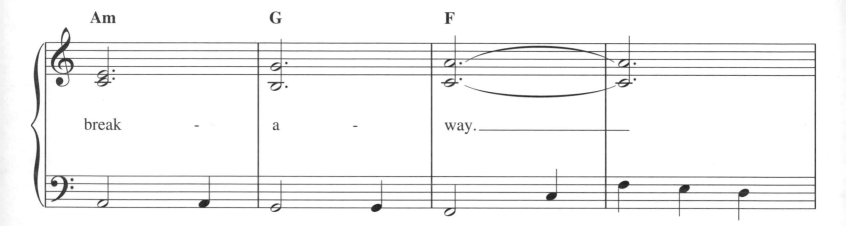

Am   **G**   **F**

break - a - way.

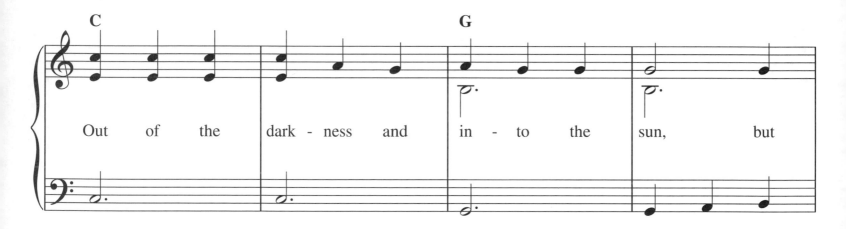

C   **G**

Out of the dark - ness and   in - to the   sun,   but

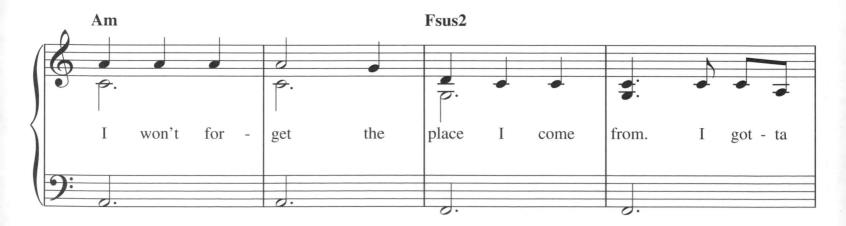

Am   **Fsus2**

I won't for - get the   place I come   from.   I got - ta

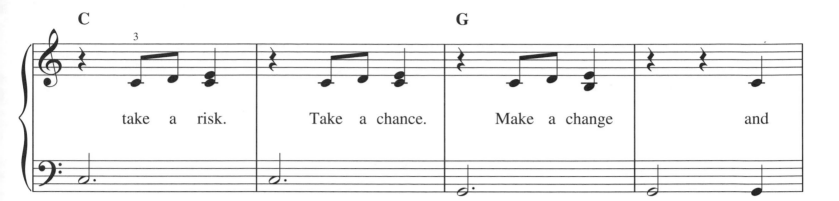

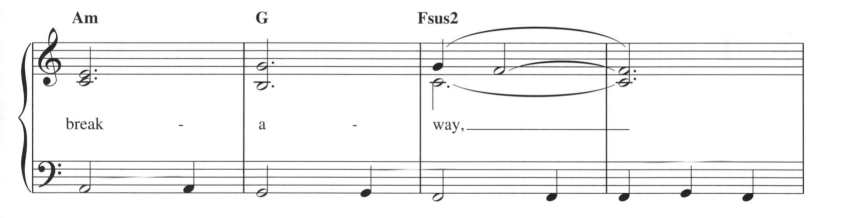

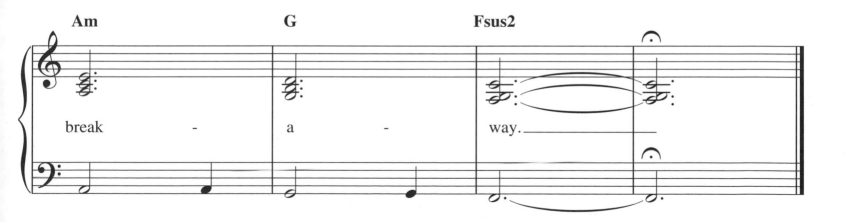

DON'T YOU WANNA STAY

Words and Music by JASON SELLERS,
PAUL JENKINS and ANDREW GIBSON

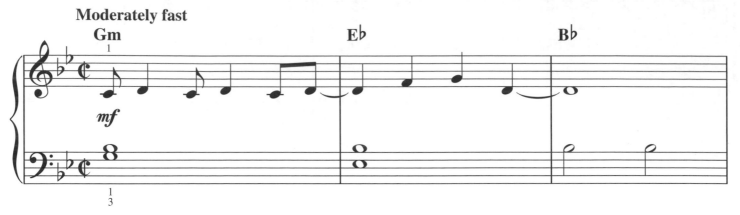

I real - ly hate to let ___
Let't take it slow. I don't ___

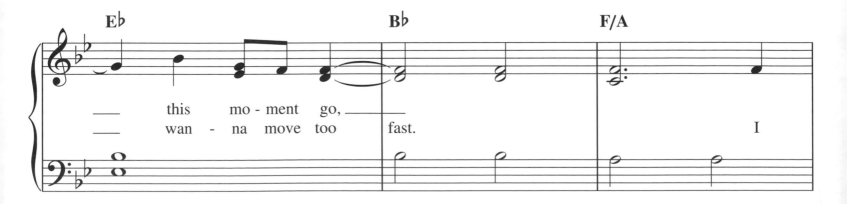

this mo - ment go, ___
wan - na move too fast.

I

touch-in' your skin and your ___ hair fall-in' slow,
don't wan - na just make love. ___ I wan-na make love last.

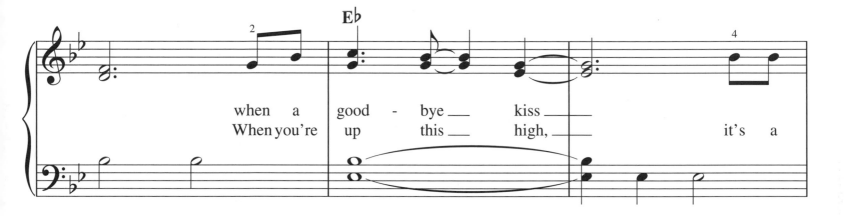

when a good - bye ___ kiss ___ it's a
When you're up this ___ high, ___

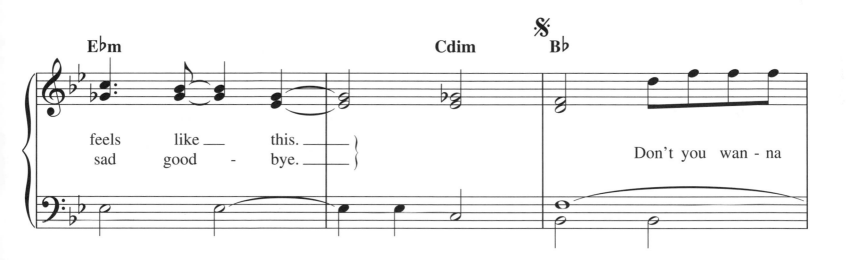

feels like ___ this. ___ Don't you wan - na
sad good - bye. ___

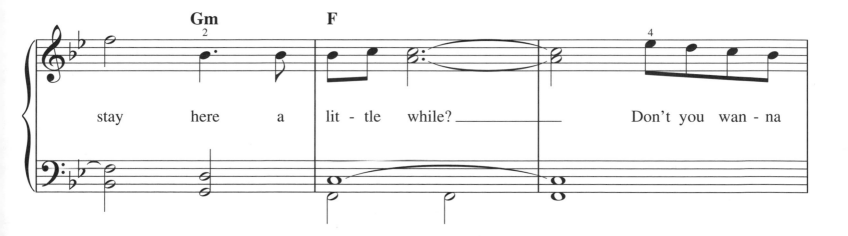

stay here a lit - tle while? ___ Don't you wan - na

hold each oth - er tight? ____ Don't you wan - na fall a - sleep __ with me __

____ to - night? _____ Don't you wan - na stay here a

lit - tle while? We can make for - ev - er feel __ this

way. ____ Don't you wan - na stay? ____

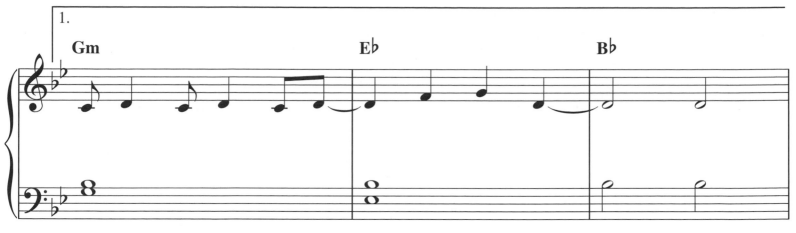

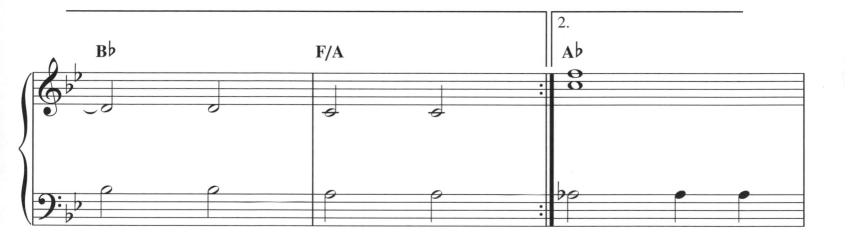

Oh, it feels___ so per - fect, ba - by. Yeah, it feels___

___ so per - fect, ba - - - by. _____

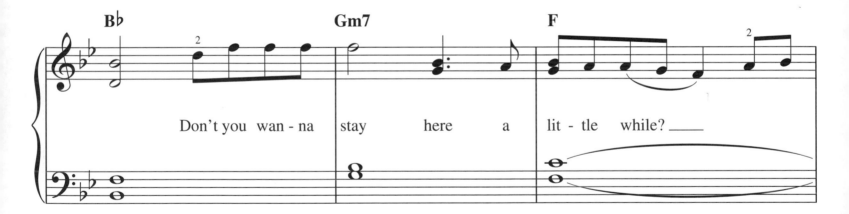

Don't you wan - na stay here a lit - tle while? _____

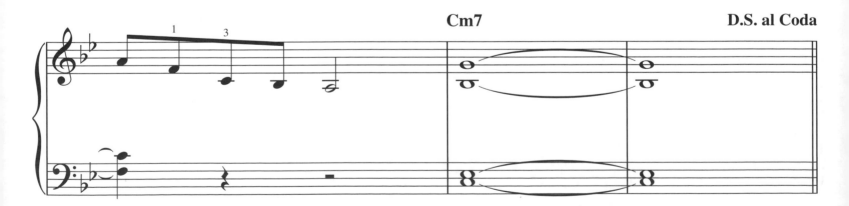

D.S. al Coda

CODA

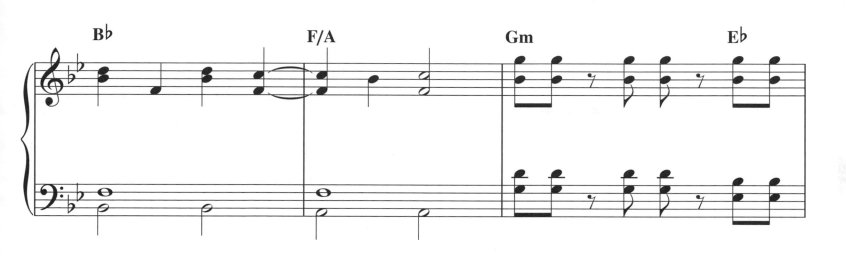

WALK AWAY

Words and Music by KELLY CLARKSON, CHANTAL KREVIAZUK,
RAINE MAIDA and KARA DioGUARDI

Moderately fast

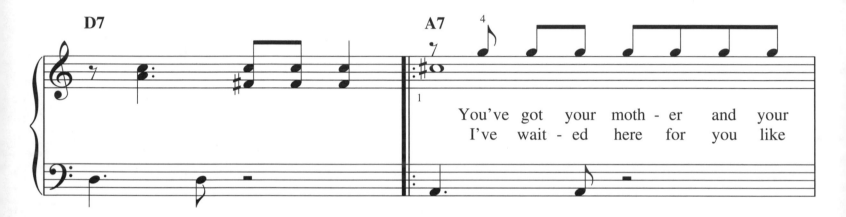

You've got your moth-er and your
I've wait-ed here for you like

broth-er, ev-'ry oth-er un-der-cov-er tell-ing you what to say.
a kid wait-ing af-ter school, so tell me how come you nev-er showed?

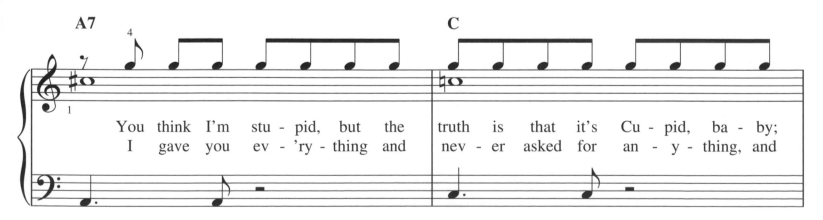

You think I'm stu-pid, but the truth is that it's Cu-pid, ba-by;
I gave you ev-'ry-thing and nev-er asked for an-y-thing, and

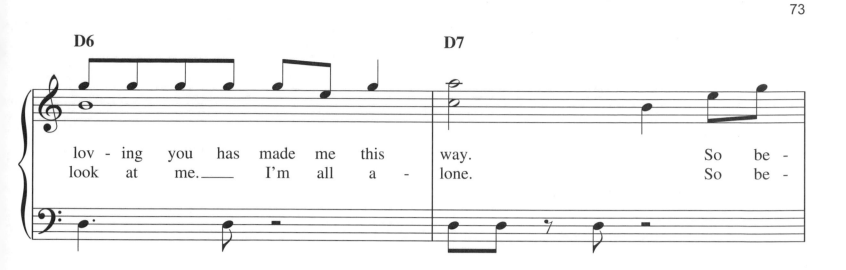

D6 ... **D7**

lov - ing you has made me this way. So be -
look at me.___ I'm all a - lone. So be -

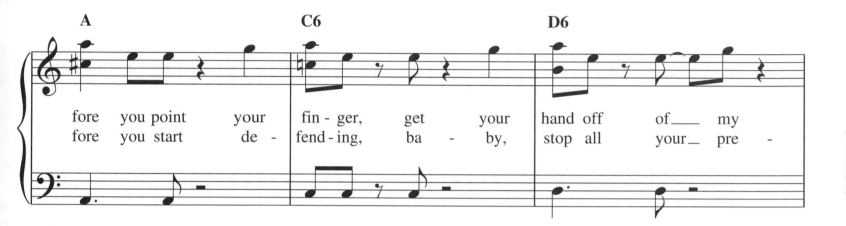

A ... **C6** ... **D6**

fore you point your fin - ger, get your hand off of___ my
fore you start de - fend - ing, ba - by, stop all your__ pre -

D7 ... **A7**

trig - ger. Oh yeah._____ You need to know the sit - u -
tend - ing. I know you know I know, so

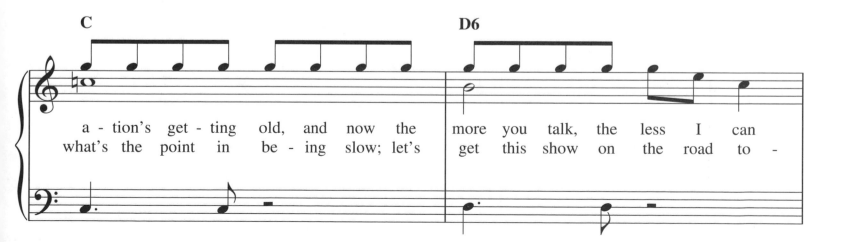

C ... **D6**

a - tion's get - ting old, and now the more you talk, the less I can
what's the point in be - ing slow; let's get this show on the road to -

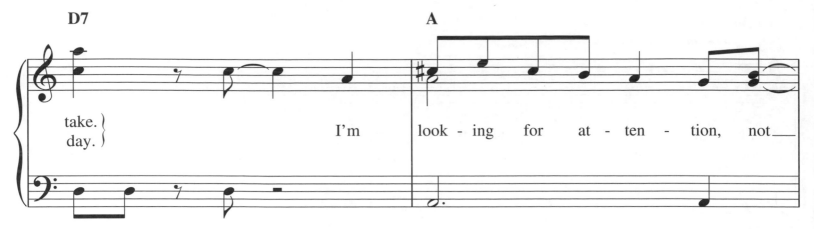

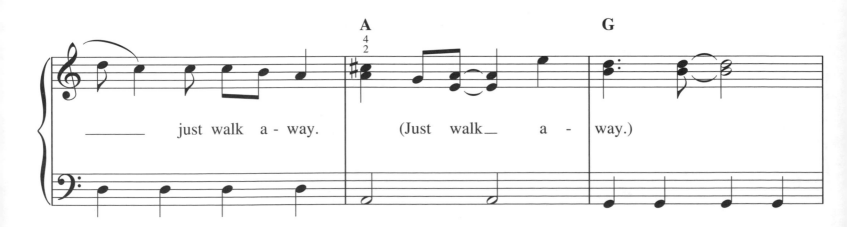

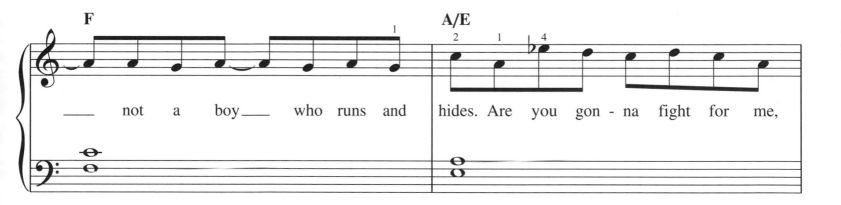

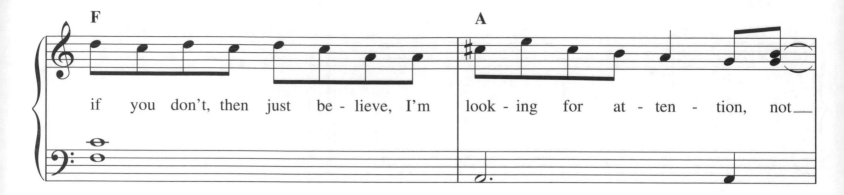

F　　　　　　　　　　　　　　　**A**

if you don't, then just be - lieve, I'm looking for at - ten - tion, not

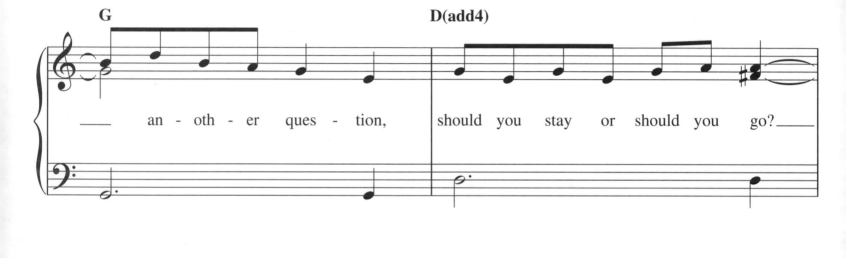

G　　　　　　　　　　　　　　　**D(add4)**

____ an - oth - er ques - tion, should you stay or should you go?____

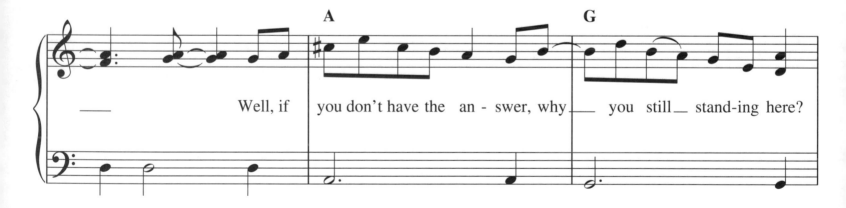

　　　　　　　　　　　　A　　　　　　　　　　　**G**

____ Well, if you don't have the an - swer, why____ you still____ stand-ing here?

D(add4)　　　　　　　　　　　　　　　　**A**

Hey, hey, hey, hey,____ just walk a - way. If you don't have the an - swer,____

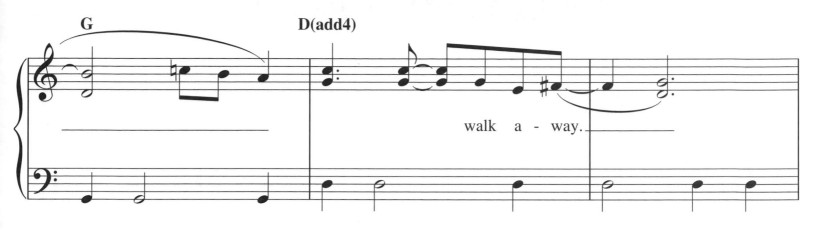

CATCH MY BREATH

Words and Music by KELLY CLARKSON,
JASON HALBERT and ERIC OLSON

Moderate Dance beat

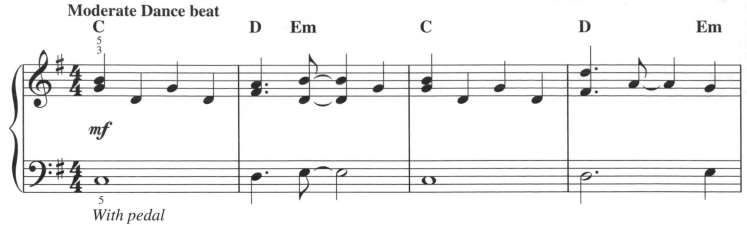

With pedal

I don't want to be left

be - hind. I found,
Dis - tance was a friend of mine.
heav - y heart, now a weight - less cloud.

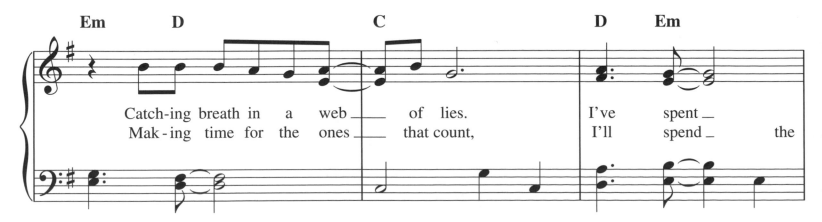

Catch-ing breath in a web of lies. I've spent
Mak-ing time for the ones that count, I'll spend the

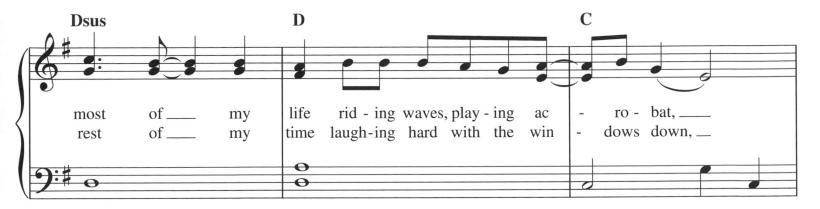

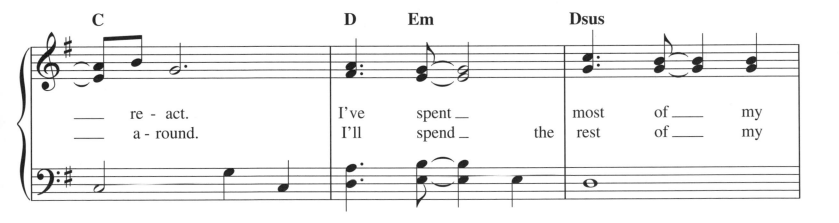

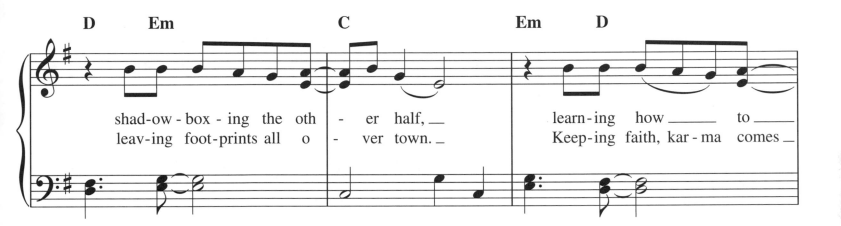

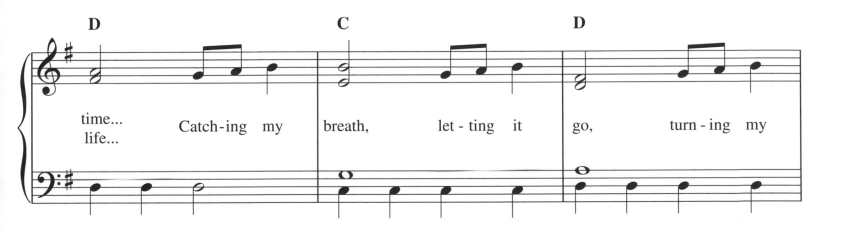

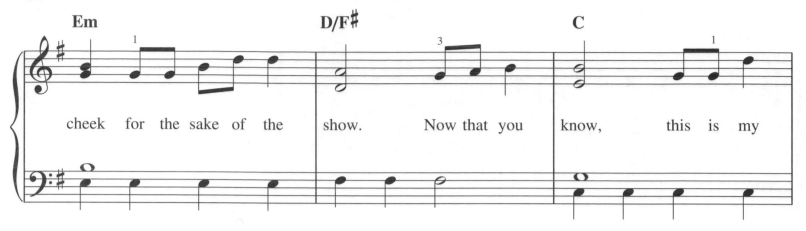

cheek for the sake of the   show.   Now that you   know,   this is my

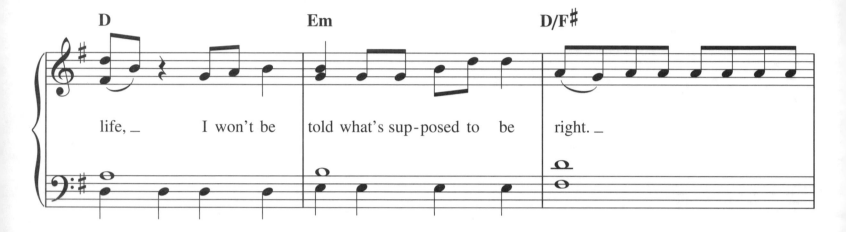

life, _   I won't be   told what's sup-posed to be   right. _

Catch my _ breath, _   no one can hold me back. _   I ain't got time for that. _

Catch my _ breath, _   won't let 'em get me down. _

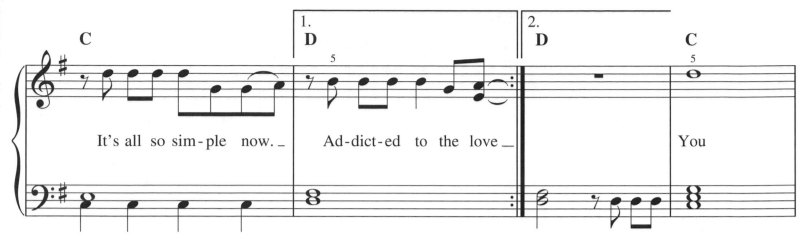

It's all so sim-ple now. _ Ad-dict-ed to the love _ You

helped me see _ the beau - ty in

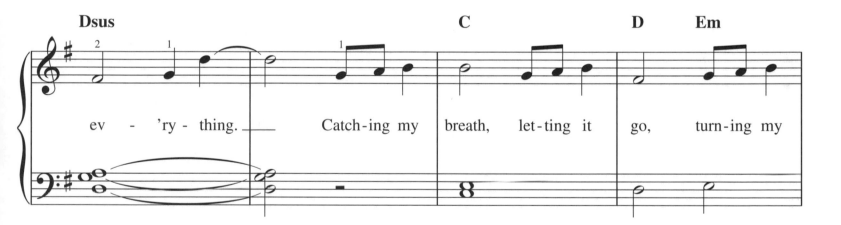

ev - 'ry - thing. _ Catch-ing my breath, let-ting it go, turn-ing my

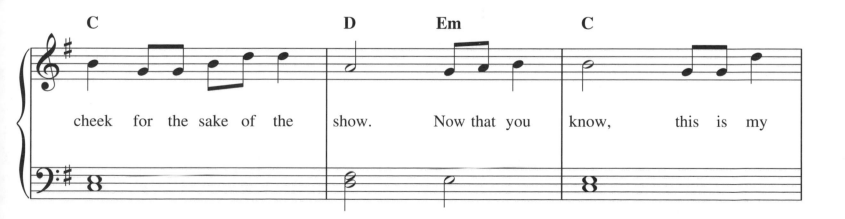

cheek for the sake of the show. Now that you know, this is my

82

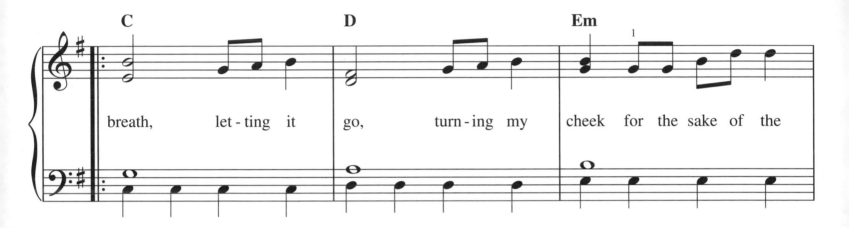

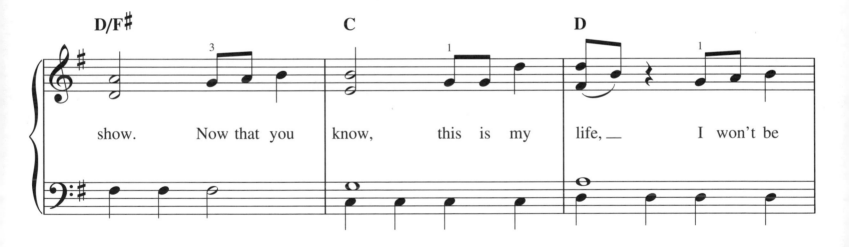

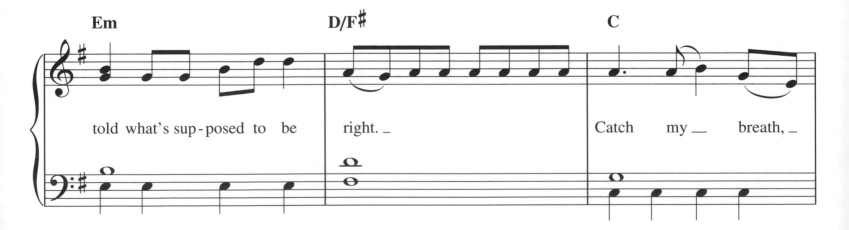

no one can hold me back. _   I ain't got time for that. _

Catch my _ breath, _   won't let 'em get me down. _   It's all so sim-ple now. _

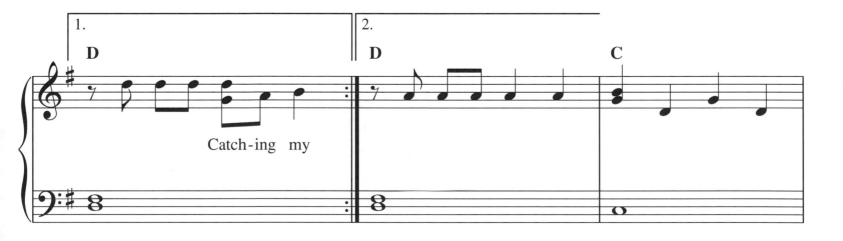

1.   2.

Catch-ing my

rit.

PEOPLE LIKE US

Words and Music by JAMES MICHAEL,
MEGHAN KABIR and BLAIR DALY

Moderately fast

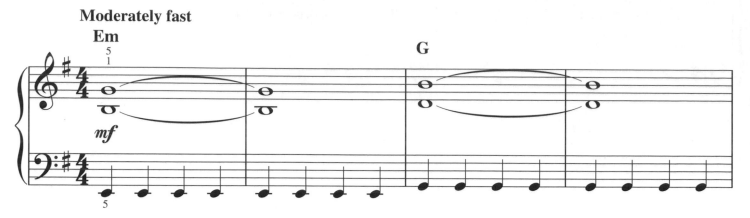

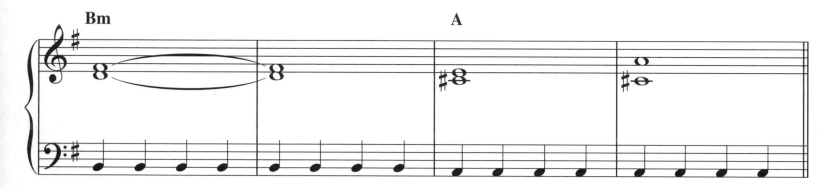

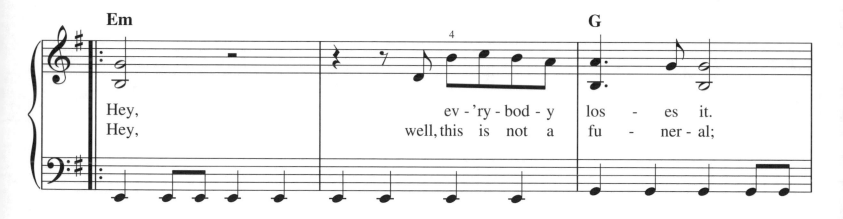

Hey,   ev - 'ry - bod - y los - es it.
Hey,   well, this is not a fu - ner - al;

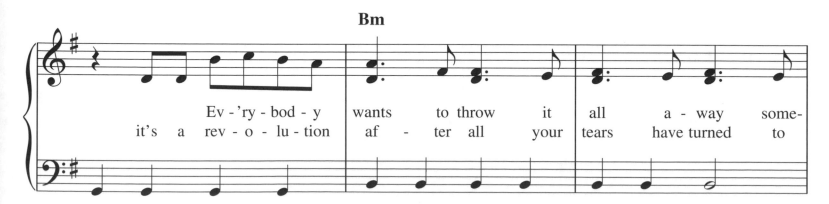

Ev - 'ry - bod - y wants to throw it all a - way some-
it's a rev - o - lu - tion af - ter all your tears have turned to

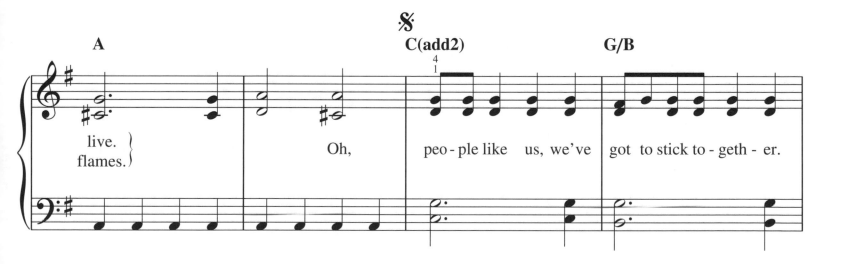

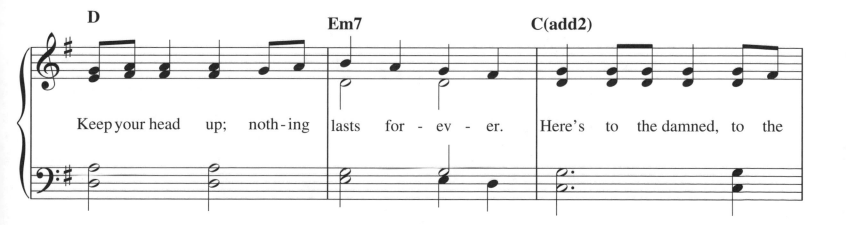

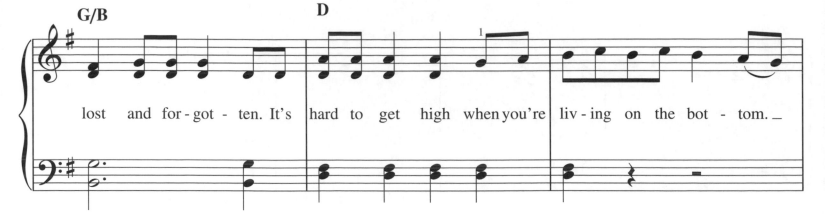

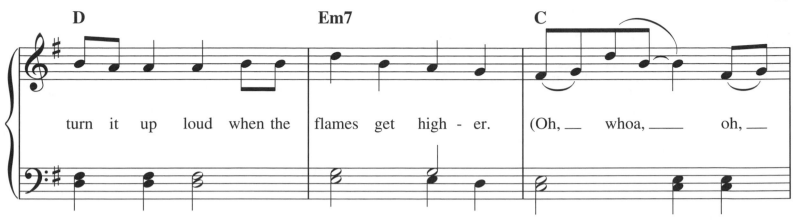

turn it up loud when the flames get high - er. (Oh, __ whoa, ___ oh, __

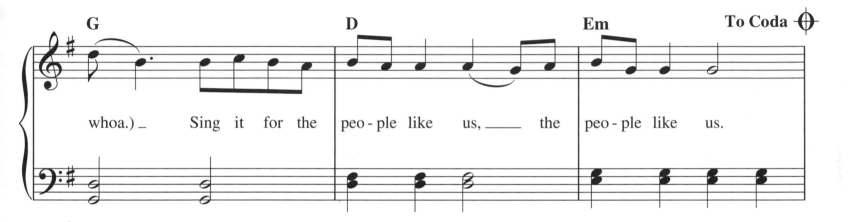

whoa.) _ Sing it for the peo - ple like us, ___ the peo - ple like us.

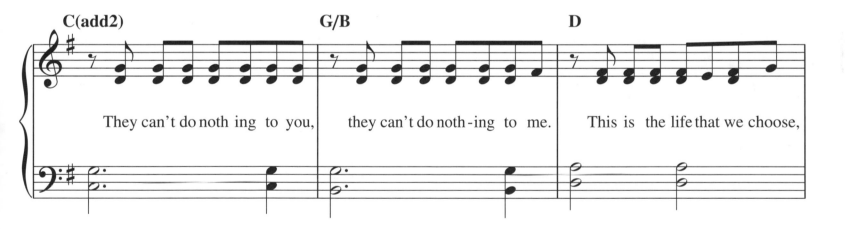

They can't do noth ing to you, they can't do noth-ing to me. This is the life that we choose,

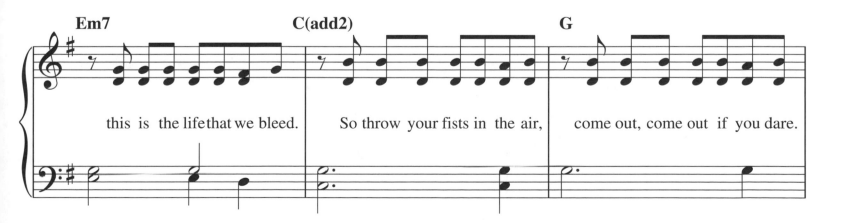

this is the life that we bleed. So throw your fists in the air, come out, come out if you dare.

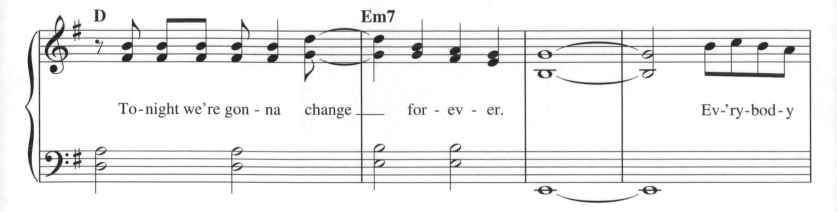

To-night we're gon - na change ___ for - ev - er. Ev-'ry-bod-y

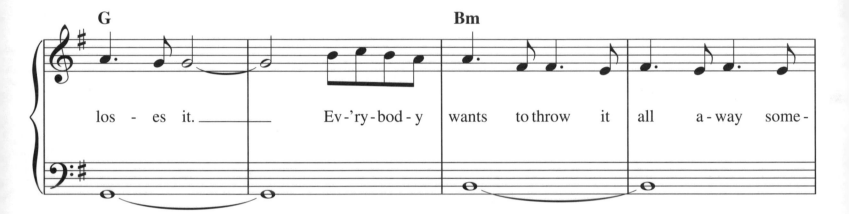

los - es it. ___ Ev-'ry-bod-y wants to throw it all a - way some-

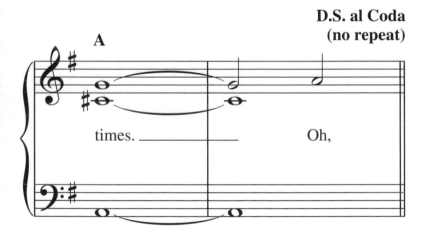

times. ___ Oh,

D.S. al Coda
(no repeat)

CODA

(Oh, ___ whoa, ___ oh, ___

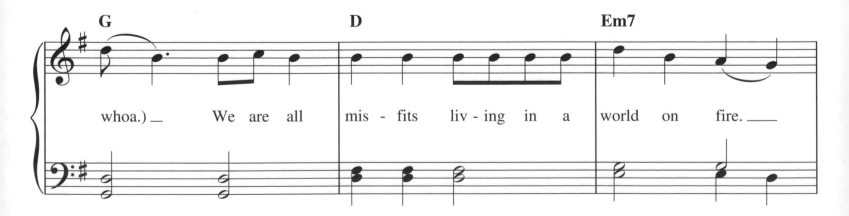

whoa.) ___ We are all mis - fits liv-ing in a world on fire. ___

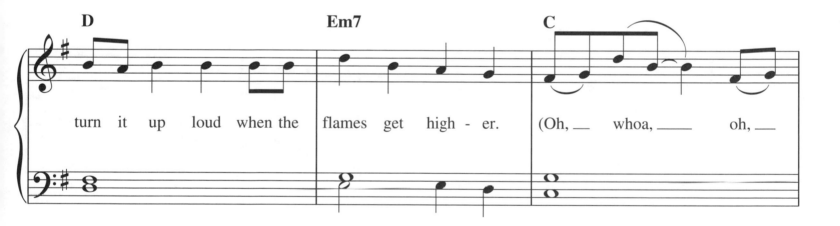

DON'T RUSH

Words and Music by LINSAY CHAPMAN,
NATALIE HEMBY and BLU SANDERS

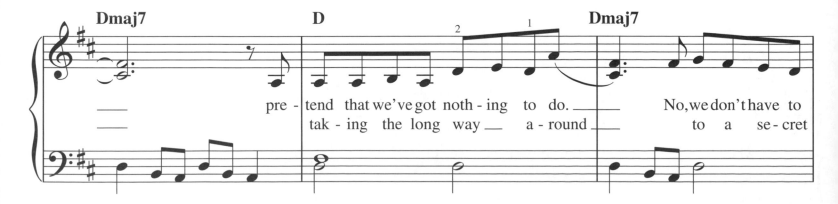

Let's wake up in the af - ter - noon, _
Throw - ing the map out the win - dow. _

_ pre - tend that we've got noth - ing to do. _ No, we don't have to
_ tak - ing the long way _ a - round _ to a se - cret

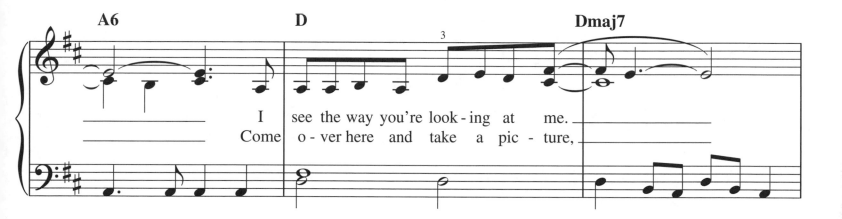

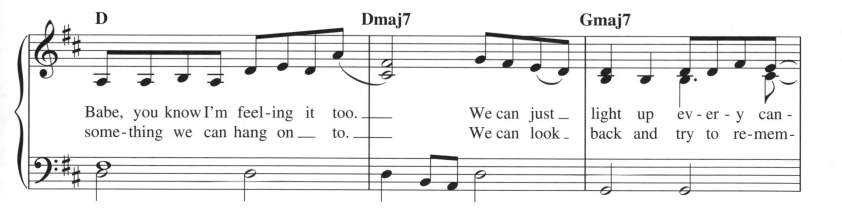

Stop-ping ev-'ry min-ute just be-cause you're in it, wish-ing ev-'ry day was

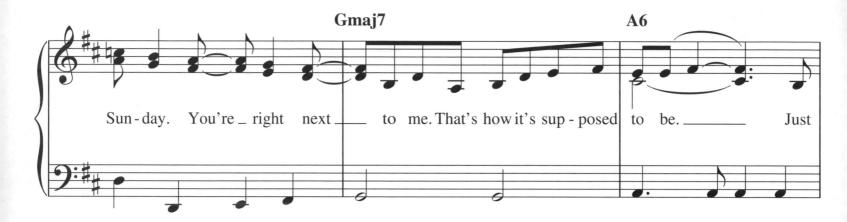

Sun-day. You're right next to me. That's how it's sup-posed to be. Just

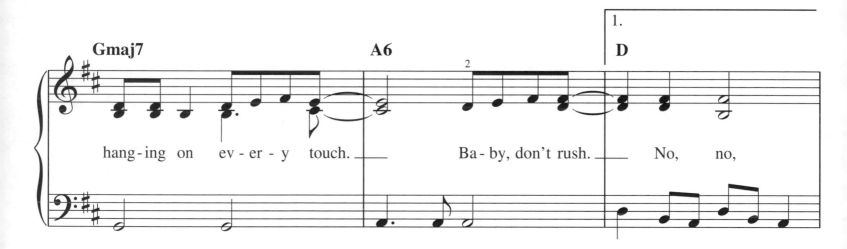

hang-ing on ev-er-y touch. Ba-by, don't rush. No, no,

ba-by, don't rush.

Stop-ping ev-'ry min-ute   just be-cause you're in   it,   wish-ing ev-'ry day was

Sun-day.   You're right   next   to me. That's how it's sup-posed to   be.

Stop-ping ev-'ry min-ute   just be-cause you're in   it,   wish-ing ev-'ry day was

Sun-day. You're right next to me. That's how it's sup-posed to be, _____ just

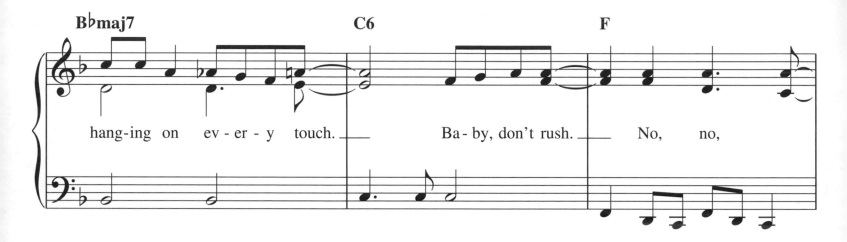

hang-ing on ev-er-y touch. _____ Ba-by, don't rush. _____ No, no,

ba-by don't rush. _____ Ba-by, don't rush. _

_ No, no, ba-by, don't rush. _____

A MOMENT LIKE THIS

Words and Music by JOHN REID
and JORGEN KJELL ELOFSSON

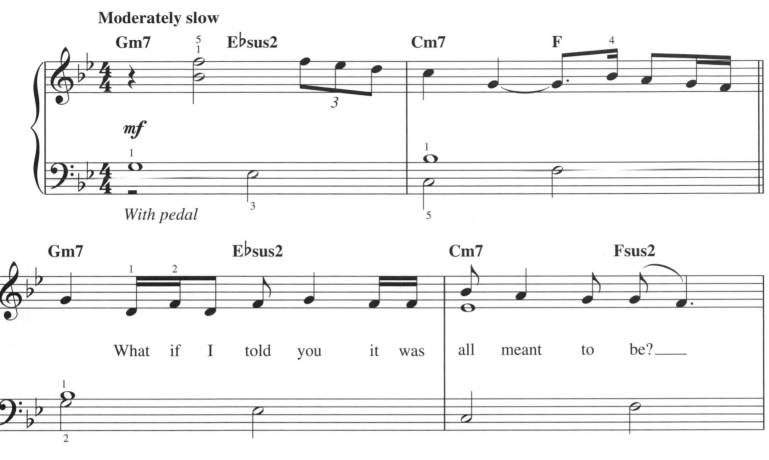

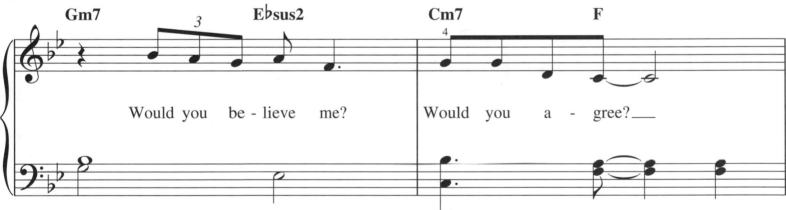

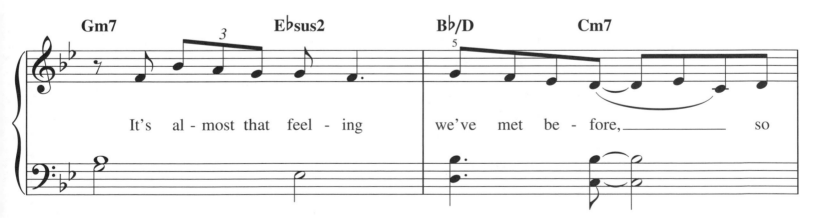

tell me that___ you don't___ think I'm | cra - zy_____ when I

tell you love_ has come_ here and | now. A mo - ment like

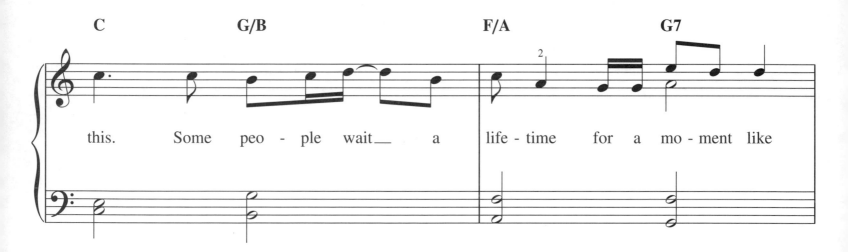

this. Some peo - ple wait__ a | life - time for a mo - ment like

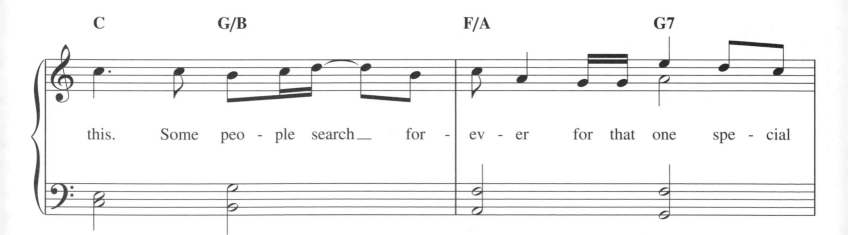

this. Some peo - ple search__ for - ev - er for that one spe - cial

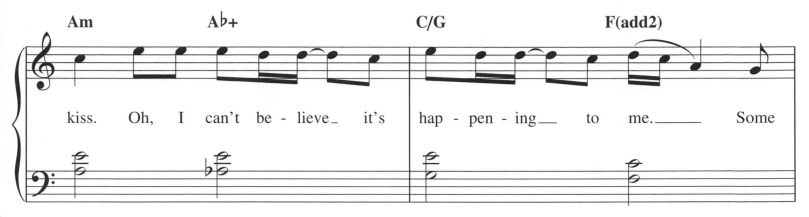

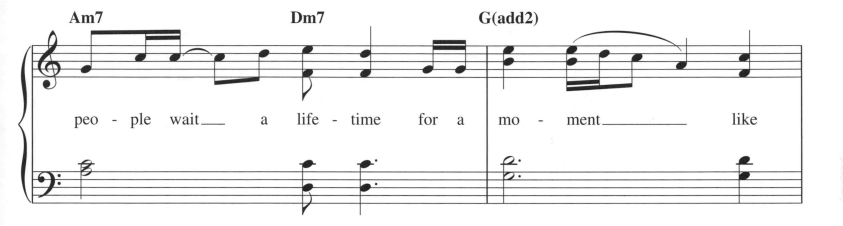

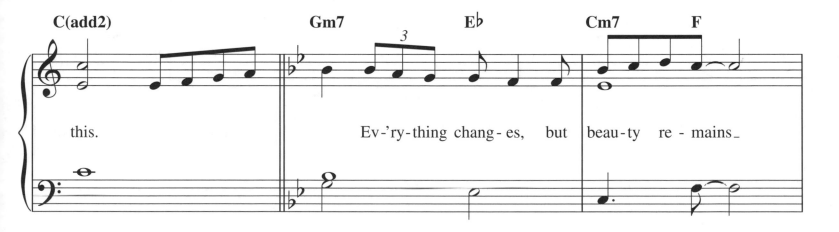

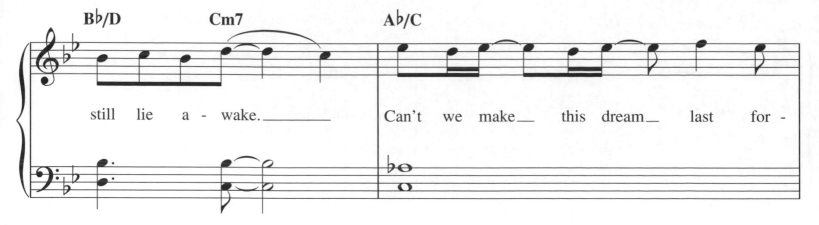

Bb/D   **Cm7**   **Ab/C**

still lie a - wake._____ Can't we make__ this dream__ last for -

Eb(add2)   **Cm7**

ev - er?___ And I'll cher - ish all__ the love_____ we

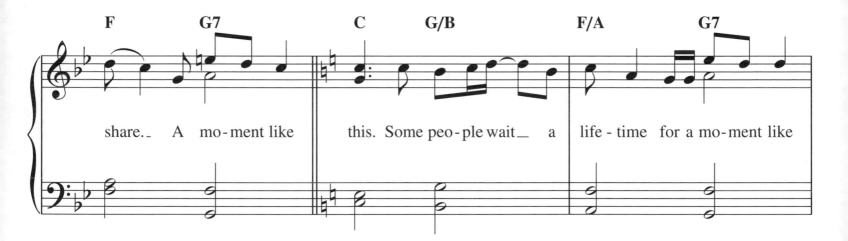

F   **G7**   **C**   **G/B**   **F/A**   **G7**

share._ A mo-ment like this. Some peo-ple wait__ a life - time for a mo-ment like

C   **G/B**   **F/A**   **G7**   **Am**   **Ab+**

this. Some peo - ple search_ for - ev - er for that one spe - cial kiss. Oh, I can't be - lieve_ it's

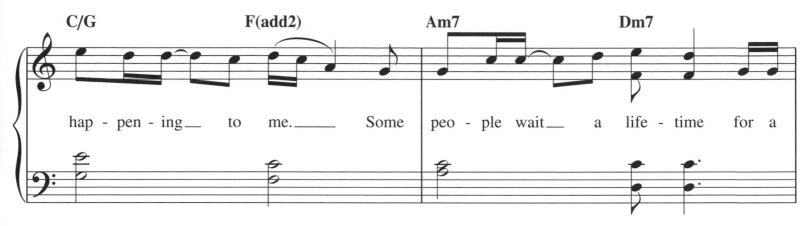

hap-pen-ing___ to me.___ Some peo-ple wait___ a life-time for a

mo-ment___ like this. Could this be___ the great-est love___ of

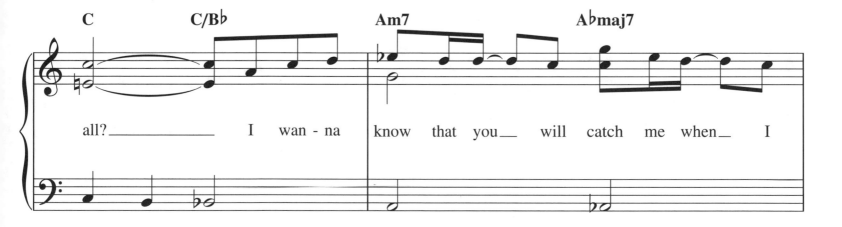

all?___ I wan-na know that you___ will catch me when___ I

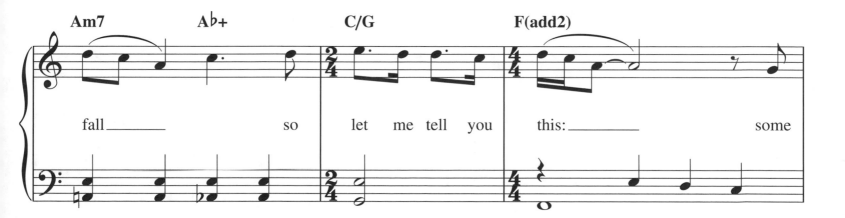

fall___ so let me tell you this:___ some

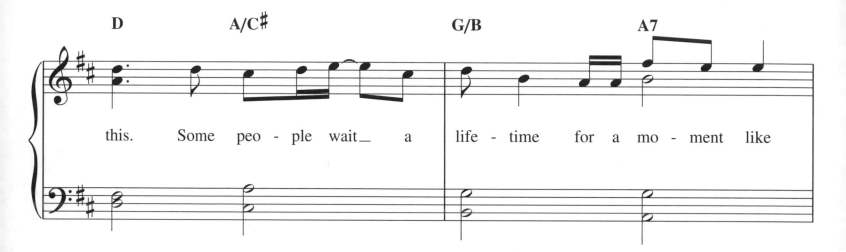

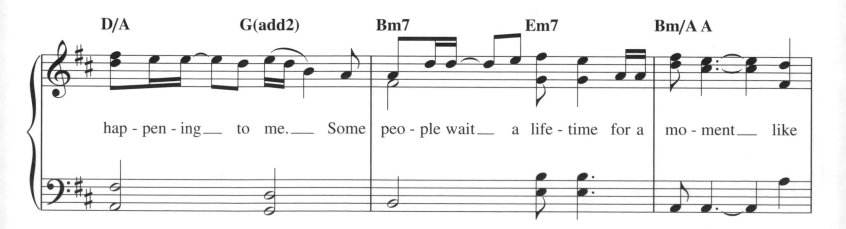

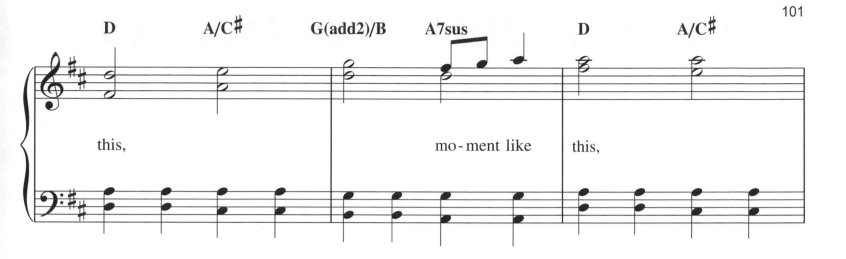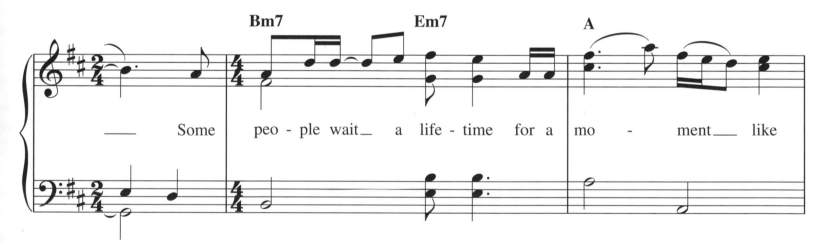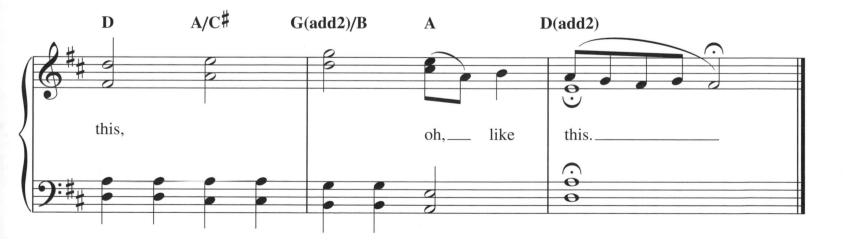

I'LL BE HOME FOR CHRISTMAS

Words and Music by KIM GANNON
and WALTER KENT

I'll   be   home   for   Christ - mas. ___

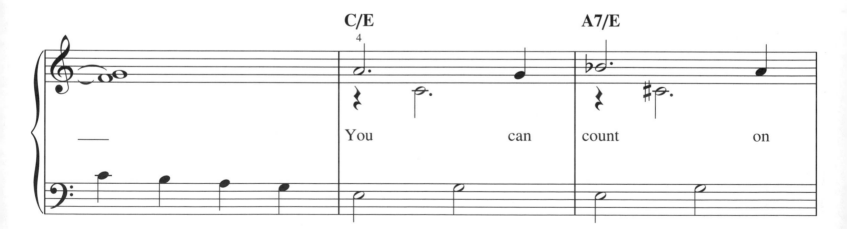

___   You   can   count   on

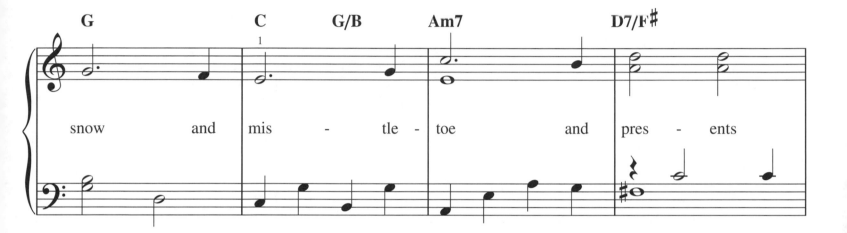

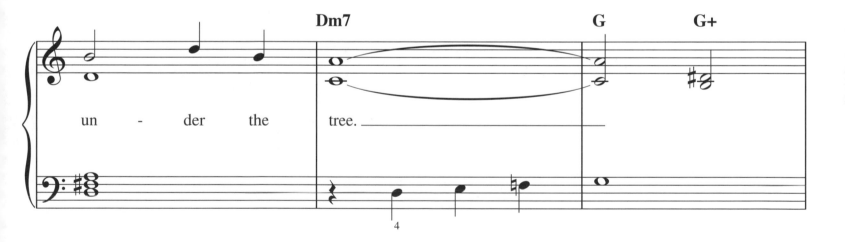

104

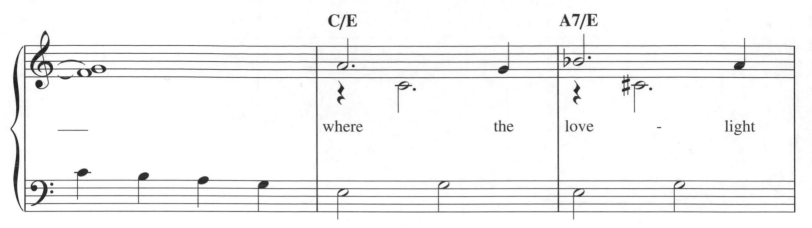

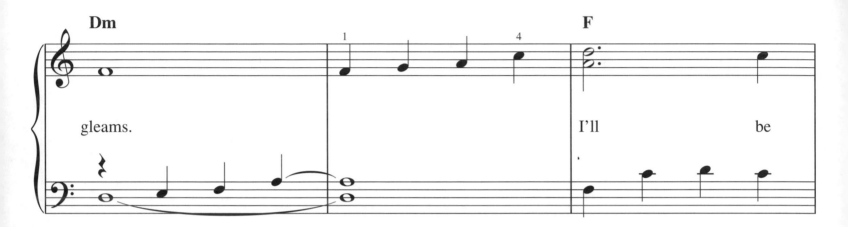

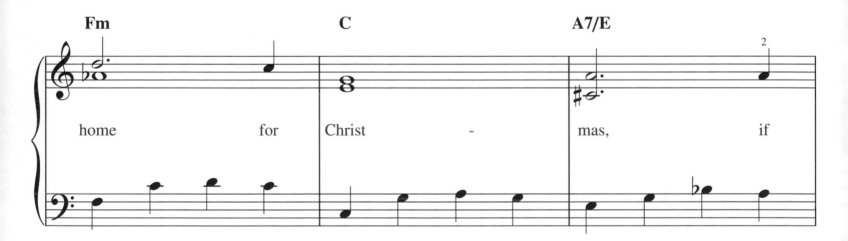